DATE DUE

The messy
quest
for meaning

"What should I do? Who am I meant to become? Deftly using his own life as a springboard to understanding Catholic traditions of 'discernment,' Stephen Martin helps readers discover answers to those two central questions. Invitingly honest, often provocative, and unfailingly useful, *The Messy Quest for Meaning* is a boon to anyone who seeks answers to questions of vocation and identity, so as to enter more deeply into a relationship with God, the fulfillment of all our longings."

Rev. James Martin, S.J.
Author of *Between Heaven and Mirth*

"What distinguishes this book is the author's new, refreshing voice. The honesty and humility with which Martin tells his own story of seeking his vocation shows enough hard-earned wisdom to make him a credible guide for readers of any age. And the surprise of his pitch-perfect humor adds to the book's rare depth, which in this era of 'spirituality lite' makes his words and ideas memorable. Do yourself a favor and read this book."

Karen Sue Smith
Editorial Director
America

"With great intelligence, wisdom, and humor, this book confronts the sheer terrifying freedom of having too many choices of what to do with our lives. From Trappist monks, saints, artists, and ex-NBA stars, among others, Martin derives practical advice that is rooted in a sense of attentiveness to our deepest desires. This book is unfailingly honest and full of real struggle, not pat answers. In the end, it is a book not just about the narrow sense of vocation—what kind of job to do—but about how to live a good life."

William T. Cavanaugh
Professor of Theology
DePaul University

"Stephen Martin reminds us that, although we may feel mired in the muck of daily details, God calls us to be about God's holy work. And, surprisingly, even at those times when we can least be expected to, we answer. I am as fond of the phrase 'messy quest' as I am of this gently helpful book. Martin reassures us that the messy side of life can be a cleanly spiritual place to live."

Valerie Schultz
Author of Closer: Musings on Intimacy, Marriage, and God

FIVE Catholic Practices FOR Finding YOUR Vocation

The messy quest for meaning

Stephen Martin

SORIN BOOKS Notre Dame, Indiana

To Dawn, Evan, and Elly

www.sorinbooks.com

Paperback: ISBN-10 1-933495-32-4   ISBN-13 978-1-933495-32-3

E-book: ISBN-10 1-933495-52-9   ISBN-13 978-1-933495-52-1

Cover image © jstan / Veer.

Cover and text design by John R. Carson.

Printed and bound in the United States of America.

Library of Congress Cataloging-in-Publication Data

Martin, Stephen.
  The messy quest for meaning : five Catholic practices for finding your vocation / Stephen Martin.
     p. cm.
  Includes bibliographical references.
  ISBN 978-1-933495-32-3 (pbk.) -- ISBN 1-933495-32-4 (pbk.)
  1. Vocation--Catholic Church. 2. Work--Religious aspects--Catholic Church. I. Title.
  BX1795.W67M37 2011
  248.4'82--dc23
                    2011045294

Contents

Foreword

AMONG THE INSPIRING TALES OF VOCATION IN
this book is one about the great French artist Henri Matisse.
Sick and in pain in his seventies, Matisse was too weak
to paint. But as an artist, he was incapable of doing nothing, so he drew. Then from his bed and his wheelchair, he
began to cut shapes from colored paper, fashioning some
of his greatest masterpieces. He also undertook his crowning achievement—the design and construction of a stunning Catholic chapel in the south of France. A childhood
friend who visited Matisse during these years attributed
the artist's youthfulness and extraordinary productivity
to his sense of purpose. I would agree, but would use the
word "vocation" to explain the source of that purpose.
While Matisse found his calling early on, sticking with it
made it possible to achieve more than he might ever have
dreamed. And through this calling Matisse regularly gathered around him a community of other artists, models, and
assistants, all of whom proved essential to his art during
that the last decade of his life.

In these pages, Stephen Martin vividly shares his own
personal experiences with the demands and opportunities
of pursuing a vocation, revealing his passion and gifted-
ness as a writer. Most important, he focuses on a key point
of Catholic spirituality—that God calls each of us to be and
to do that which only we can be and do.

We are each called to holiness in a way unique to ourselves, because we are unique creations of God and because

our vocation is built on the deepest desires God has seeded within us. One needn't be a saint or a genius (like Matisse) to pursue a vocation, Stephen assures us. Which politely reminds us that we have no excuse for not trying to heed God's voice.

I give Stephen enormous credit for suggesting more than once in a book full of good humor and lively characters that the pursuit of vocation is difficult, that one will need to work as hard and as persistently as the saints and our other heroes have done. It is Jesus, after all, whom we follow. We may face obstacles as great as those that caused others to stumble. Yet the promise of vocation is life's highest good. A life true to the call of God as best we understand it will be filled with purpose, with meaning. That life is its own reward. This book provides many examples of different types of people who have followed God's call to pursue a vocation, companions who will no doubt inspire you to get started, or to keep going, or to start over. For a vocation, just like a commitment to love someone, is an ongoing choice that must be renewed over and over at critical junctures in life.

That understanding of vocation, Stephen says, is countercultural. For in the United States today, we typically think of vocation as something teens or twenty-somethings decide on as they first consider a career and other lifestyle choices. But these decisions are not one-time choices. People often complete years of education and devote themselves to a career, before they realize it is not what they had hoped and not even close to their deepest desires. Think bigger. Not merely about your job but your reason for being, for getting up in the morning on your darkest days—that comes closer to what vocation means in the

Christian sense. What is God calling me to do and to be? is a question that recurs throughout one's lifelong quest for meaning. That question may be prompted by an accident, a tragedy or a failure, by an event like the children leaving home or returning, or by unbidden opportunities, new interests or retirement. At all such times and also at regular intervals, Stephen urges us to give ourselves a spiritual check-up by assessing our vocation.

I find this book to be important and helpful, primarily because Stephen builds his reflections on five ancient Christian practices that he himself has learned from a long study of Trappist monks. Fans of Thomas Merton will recognize the Trappist wisdom running through the chapters. Naming our desires, developing focus, learning humility, cultivating community and exploring the margins of our inner and outer lives are time-tested spiritual disciplines for people of every age. These practices require diligence and patience, but the effort develops discernment and stamina and can bring great joy. Vocation, however, is not merely a path to personal fulfillment and happiness, though that may result from having accepted God's call. Rather, that call is an invitation to join in the divine work of healing a broken world. If that sounds too difficult, too vague or too theological, don't worry. Just try the first practice, which asks you to name your deepest desires. God will forge the link between those desires and the healing acts this world needs from you.

Karen Sue Smith

Introduction

"BOBBY HURLEY NEARLY RAN OVER ME LAST WEEK!" a female classmate chirped as we stepped out of class into a bright September afternoon. Rather than expressing relief that she had avoided being struck by a vehicle, she actually seemed a little sorry she hadn't ended up on the hood. The reason was obvious enough: he might have noticed her then—and back in the fall of 1991, few things meant more to students at Duke University than a mere glance from Bobby Hurley.

As the school's sensational point guard, Hurley had led Duke's basketball team to its first national champion-ship just five months before. By April of the following year, he would be a full-fledged hero—featured on the cover of *Sports Illustrated*, Most Valuable Player of the Final Four, the spark behind the Blue Devils' second straight NCAA title. I didn't even know the guy and had never seen him driving. But during my freshman year at Duke, there was no one I envied more than Bobby Hurley.

My jealousy wasn't new either. In fact, it was in full flower before I'd even set foot on campus, back when I was a third-string distance runner on my high school track team. Hurley, fresh off a legendary career at St. Anthony High in Jersey City, was already a star in the making at Duke. Here was a guy who had everything I didn't have—athletic prowess, fame, and, judging by the rumor mill, all the women he could handle. He also apparently had the one thing I did have—book smarts. A basketball magazine

I'd leafed through once mentioned something about his stellar grade point average.

When my uncle, a Capuchin priest from Pittsburgh, stopped by the house one night for dinner, I greeted him with a plateful of teenage aggrievement. Why, I demanded, still smarting from the humiliation of the previous year's biweekly acne treatments, did God give one guy so much? Why couldn't I be like Hurley?

My uncle, calm and thoughtful, nodded slowly. "Hmm," he said. "The distribution of talent. That's a difficult one."

"The distribution of what?" I nearly shouted in the midst of my outrage. "Must the Catholic Church have a theological construct for everything?"

My uncle gently explained that God endows us all with gifts; it's our lifelong challenge to ascertain what they are and how to use them. We waste our time—and stray farther away from our own purpose—by envying other talents God never even intended us to have. From the distance of twenty years and some additional maturity on my part, his answer makes much more sense now than it did then. Snared as I was, however, in the clutches of bleak novels about the meaninglessness of life by Hemingway, Fitzgerald, Camus, and other chronically unhappy philosophers and writers, not to mention self-pity and tremendous yearning for several girls I was too shy to ask out, I nodded, dismissed his advice out of hand, and continued on my bitter way. Many years and some developed talent later, I do take solace in this: there was a good reason to be jealous of Bobby Hurley. He did have something I didn't have. But it wasn't any of the things I thought it was.

It's taken most of my adult life to figure that out—and, fittingly, it was my Capuchin uncle who put me on the scent. Chatting at a family reunion several years ago, we touched on the shortage of priests. Vocations were still out there, my uncle told me. But our culture had gotten noisy and distracting, and it was getting harder and harder to hear the call. Making matters worse, most of us had also forgotten how to slow down long enough to listen. And it wasn't just potential priests who were missing out. Increasingly, people in general couldn't get a grip on who they were supposed to be. Even the simple notion of a calling, emanating from deep within and filling our day-to-day lives with meaning, seemed foreign to many of us. Instead, from our earliest days in school, we often pursue what others expect of us, or what we think is practical or prestigious, or whatever we fall into by accident or circumstance. Sometimes, we stumble into the right fit for our lives. Most of the time we don't—and the toll ranges from broken relationships, addictions, and physical or mental illness to burnout, creeping frustration, and the relentlessly nagging question: "Is this all there is?"

It's only recently I've understood that when you strip away the highlight reels and the championship trophies and the chants from adoring students, this was Hurley's greatest blessing: he had a calling. When he stepped on the court, he knew exactly who he was supposed to be, and he didn't want to be anyone else. He was an artist, the author of stunning no-look passes and daring drives down jam-packed lanes, uncannily threading the ball through a thicket of flailing arms and legs. More important than that, though, it was obvious how much he loved to play and how hard he worked to get better—not merely so he could make another highlight reel move, but because he owed it to himself to give every possible ounce of effort to what he was born to do. Watching him, you got the feeling he'd play precisely the same way against you in a driveway game of one-on-one, and take the same deep satisfaction in it too. A calling that pure, coupled with that kind of self-knowledge, is actually worthy of envy—now more than ever.

I believe today that regardless of the pain that sometimes comes from the lack of prestige or success in the world, such a calling is within reach for all of us. Finding and fulfilling a vocation does not require genius. It does not depend on extraordinary talent or knowing important people. It certainly has nothing to do with fame, despite our society's ever-growing fixation with it. Rather, starting with faith—in both God and the trueness of one's calling—we can stand out in our own right, instead of fixating with jealousy, regret, and bitterness on the kind of people we aren't and were never intended to be. We probably won't play out our calling in the headlines or on national television, but that doesn't matter. We're all called to live with passion and purpose in a broken world that is desperate for the very best each of us can bring. God will know when we're succeeding. So will we and the people close to us— and that is a profoundly Christian, if countercultural, way of measuring success.

Where to begin, however? How does one find one's "calling"? The Catholic Church offers numerous guides, both living and dead, who show us how to discern a call or build on the progress we've already made. They remind us, first of all, of this enduring fact: the journey toward a calling can transform our lives in ways we never imagined. In fact, embarking on it is perhaps the only way to experience life to its fullest. The pursuit of an authentic vocation can bring out the best in us and those around us, making us more self-aware, creating opportunities to serve others with our talents, enriching our days with meaning that might have eluded us before.

These guides testify, too, with even more challenge, to a second lesson: discovering one's vocation can be an extremely demanding trek. The first (and perhaps most difficult) demand is we must live with a degree of uncertainty. We don't know where the journey will lead or how long it's going to take, though we can be sure it will test our strength and demand sacrifice. How many of us have told a friend, "I just want to know what I'm supposed to do with my life"? We expect such an answer to cause everything to make sense and all anxiety disappear from that point forward. In truth, receiving the "answer," even if we receive it in a powerful, unambiguous way, is just the start. We might not—and probably won't ever—be entirely at ease with all our calling requires of us. Might it mean turning down lucrative job offers? What if it brings us skepticism or even misunderstanding and contempt from loved ones? Are we willing to end close relationships with people who think we're misguided? What if we make a mistake and need to start over?

We are social animals, wired to conform. Convention frequently drives us to pursue wealth, status, and security, not because we are vain (although we can be), but because the alternative can be deeply frightening. Unfortunately, the work that brings us the reward of security is often not the work that makes the best use of our gifts (although sometimes it can). Even if we don't necessarily crave the rewards that come with following the path of security (although sometimes we do), we oftentimes conform merely because it's what our culture expects us to do, and to challenge that is frightening. Discovering a vocation is difficult because we need to both construct and *trust* an inner compass instead of the outer one by which we've oriented much of our lives. In America, living out a calling, whether it leads us to riches or rags, is a countercultural act. If we are ever to get to a true calling, we need to be intentional—the more, the better.

In this book, I explore five steps, grounded in the Catholic tradition, that provide a practical road map for moving ahead. They involve naming our desires, developing focus, learning humility, cultivating community, and exploring the margins of our inner and outer lives.

Why these five, and what is the basis for them? They emerged in part through much reflection over the past decade on my own experiences—lessons shared by friends and mentors, interviews and observations I continue to compile as a journalist, and particularly through the ordeal of a serious illness in my mid twenties. Just as significantly, these practices are strongly informed by the Christian mystical tradition, specifically the wisdom and routines of Trappist monks. Since my first visit to a monastery in college, the Trappist way of life—so completely counter to our prevailing culture in virtually every way—has proved an endless source of fascination. Over the years, I've made many retreats to monasteries, interviewed monks, read their books, and closely studied their way of life. Every page of this book is, in some way, rooted in the Trappist spirit and example.

Examining exactly how we build a vocation and what examples of success look like are the central business of the book. Going in search of a call, as you will see, is an adventure of the highest order, and it exacts a real price. In fact, it must—because for many of us a call is created in the very act of paying for it. Even Bobby Hurley wasn't exempt from this reality.

After Duke, Hurley was drafted by the NBA's Sacramento Kings. Heading home from a game one December night during his rookie season, he turned at a dark intersection. Another car—charging down the road at sixty miles an hour with its headlights off—broadsided him. Not wearing a seatbelt, Hurley flew one hundred feet into a ditch. He'd likely have died if a teammate hadn't happened upon the scene just minutes later and called for help. Even so, Hurley's injuries were staggering: two collapsed lungs, a fractured shoulder blade, a damaged knee, and, most seriously, a torn windpipe. The accident shattered his body and very nearly killed him. His grueling recovery and return to pro basketball a year later made great headlines. But Hurley's body and his game were never quite the same. He did not become an NBA superstar and was out of the league within five years.

Back in those pre-Internet days, it wasn't easy to keep up with his whereabouts. Besides, freshly out of college and struggling mightily with my own purpose, I was too busy to think about anyone but myself. Sometimes Hurley's name would pop up in a box score on the sports page, or a sportscaster might bring his name up when a Duke game was on television. As the years went on, an article about him would appear now and then. It seemed he lamented his lost career. His focus had drifted. He'd found some peace training and breeding racehorses. But he still felt awkward outside the gym. Increasingly, though, I relegated him to my cluttered mental bin of college memories, my substantial capacity for schoolboy jealousy ultimately crowded out by kids, mortgage payments, and work deadlines.

Then one Saturday afternoon, not long ago, Hurley popped right back into my life. Glancing up at the television, I saw a clip for March Madness. There was Hurley, skinny and jubilant, celebrating Duke's shocking upset of previously undefeated UNLV in the 1991 Final Four. The clip faded, and suddenly there, in the center of the screen, stood the present-day, middle-aged Bobby Hurley, his dark hair thinner and his body thicker. "No way!" I thought. "That's Bobby Hurley? How did he get so old?" And then moments later: "How did I?" Poking around later for hints of what he was up to now, I came across a story from a Duke sports magazine, one of those "whatever happened to that guy?" stories about ex-jocks, the kind that often don't end well. But this was different.

Hurley, the story said, is Catholic. He didn't like to think too much about the accident that put him at death's door and stole his career. It was, he said, "a tough deal." For years afterward, he missed basketball. If he needed to settle his mind, the former all-American would shoot baskets by himself in the driveway. But at the same time, being around the game pained him, reminding him of what he'd lost. He tried working as a scout for a professional team, but that didn't last. He talked about getting into coaching but didn't. He went into the horse-breeding business instead. Still, a few years ago he told a reporter, "I can't complain. I believe God brought me back for a reason."

The reason, he said, was his wife and three young children. They became a fresh source of passion and inspiration, the new vocation of family man gradually blossoming in place of the old dream. In the time since that commercial showed up in my den, Hurley's life has taken a few more major twists. The horse-breeding business he ran in Florida fell apart. Then his younger brother Danny Hurley was hired as the head basketball coach at Wagner University in New York. One of his first moves was offering Bobby a job as an assistant coach, which he accepted. This time the timing felt right. "I need to get back in a gym," the thirty-eight-year-old Hurley told a Staten Island newspaper. He'd had his original vocation torn away from him but still managed to stumble back toward it, and it fitfully grew into a second, richly rewarding one along the way. His story is more dramatic than most of ours. But how different is it really?

We all struggle to get on the right path; it's an equally challenging fight to stay on course once we've found a calling. That's where the five core practices laid out in this book come to our aid. I know the practices explored in this book to be true because following them changed, and in some respects even saved, my life. More broadly, they have transformed the lives of Trappist monks for far longer—a thousand years, to be exact. I wrote this book to make their knowledge accessible and actionable for more of us. I wrote it, too, to make sense of my own experience and make it useful for others. I hope you find it an engaging, hands-on, and, above all, practical guide to the most important work we can do in our lives—finding and fulfilling our callings.

Part 1 recounts my own struggles to grasp a purpose, from my awkward high school and college years through the present day in which I've emerged, now in my late thirties, far more comfortable in my own skin. In part 2, the bulk of the book, we will look in detail at the five practices I've learned—and how they can help you journey toward your calling right now and well into the future.

You will see it is crucial, first of all, to follow our desires. What attracts us? What leaves us cold? This shouldn't be hard to observe, but we manage to make it hard. Since we are continually distracted by the Internet, television, and the latest hand-held devices, it's challenging to slow down long enough to identify what moves us. We're eager to get things done, check the next item off the list. But to what are we truly drawn?

Once we know our desires, we need a second trait: the focus to follow through on them, to make room in our lives for what matters most. Monks passionately desire total union with God. Unlike most of us, they don't passively await blinding moments of insight or let how they're feeling on a given day decide the outcome of their journey. Instead, they devote themselves to highly structured lives of prayer, work, and study. Might getting a little more focused in our own lives give us the momentum we need to enter more fully into our own callings?

At the same time, winding our way toward our own uniquely personal vocation means letting go of many things—preconceptions of ourselves, the opinions of others, the temptation to settle for easy answers. Letting go calls for the humility to accept where our desires lead us instead of where we want to steer ourselves. Humility is perhaps the most fundamental key to salvation in the gospels, and certainly one of the keys to finding and embracing our calling.

With humility comes the realization we're not likely to find or to fulfill our vocations solely by ourselves. Even Jesus needed his disciples. The rest of us need help as well—and we can find it in community. In fact, the pursuit of a calling can—and in my case, did—devolve into an exercise in self-absorption. So it's crucial that we involve others on our quest. They have plenty to teach us about our strengths and weaknesses. They can offer inspiration that helps us move through challenging times—and also afford us the privilege of assisting in the pursuit of their own callings. The vocational journey, after all, is not just about us. We are all, as St. Paul reminds us, part of the Body of Christ. The Church's collective progress toward salvation and the development of our unique callings as individual Christians are closely intertwined. We have critical roles to play in helping each other along.

Finally, the pursuit of our own vocations sometimes calls for journeying into the unexplored regions of our communities and, even more significantly, our own hearts, minds, and souls. Many of us lose sight of our vocations because we're too quick to follow society's conventions, which often dictate the jobs we have, the friends we make, and the views we hold. It's worth remembering that Christianity emerged entirely from the margins. Living our faith requires keeping one foot over there. That's what Mary did two thousand years ago when she said yes to God, and it's what some of our most visionary spiritual leaders do today as well. As the examples we will explore in this book remind us, when we listen less to the opinions of the world and more to God and to our own hearts, we're likely to see our vocations arise and evolve in ways we never imagined.

Let me be clear: this is not one of those volumes on "how to find a meaningful job" that a career counselor might hand you. Certainly, there's nothing wrong with those books. But there's already plenty of them out there. Instead of industry overviews, educational prerequisites, personality tests, and skill inventories, this book is grounded in a different tradition altogether—that of Christian mysticism. This book might actually help you find a specific career that is more compelling, but it's more concerned with helping you find answers to life's most fundamental questions: What was I put here to do? And how do I do it? In these pages, we'll meet ourselves where we are and see what we can learn from some of history's greatest teachers. We will ready ourselves for the next steps on our own unrepeatable journeys—not the journeys we think we should take or wish we could, but the ones to which we're called.

PART ONE

My (Messy) Catholic Quest for Meaning

CHAPTER ONE

Wilderness: A Brief History of a Breakdown

I ONCE SPENT A SUMMER IN MAYBERRY RUNNING for my life. The doctor said it was a good idea. I was a journalist at the time, paid (quite poorly) to ask follow-up questions. But hunched over in the exam room with a stack of new prescriptions clenched in my fist, there wasn't much to say to the doctor. My situation spoke for itself. Most days and too many nights, I labored in a dreary newspaper-bureau office, filing forgettable dispatches about water-main breaks, job fairs, and poisoned dogs. I shared this space with an endlessly squawking police scanner and an affable, chain-smoking circulation manager. He was exactly the kind of aw-shucks guy you might expect to meet many times over in Mount Airy, North Carolina— the town immortalized on *The Andy Griffith Show* as idyllic Mayberry.

To our left was a parole office. To our right was a boarding house full of guys destined for parole if they weren't already on it. The guy who lived in the apartment next to mine was not well. Through the kitchen wall, I sometimes heard him play the same riff from a song literally dozens of times in a row. One night he paced outside my door repeating over and over again, "The need for order. The need for order. The need for order."

Just a few months before, I'd rented a rambling apartment on South Main Street in a stately, turn-of-the-century Georgian Colonial. The house, divided into five apartments, was on the National Register of Historic Places, which was another way of saying you lived there at your own risk. I had to roll the ill-fitting window shades up by hand to let in specks of sunlight and stomp on the floor a couple times a night to keep the television focused. One night, a pillow slipped off my bed onto the baseboard heating strip behind it. By morning, it was seared with brown burn lines. But that was all part of the charm. After all, the place cost just $375 a month. It was also smack in the middle of everything that a town of eight thousand people in the middle of nowhere could offer. I could walk within minutes to work, the post office, the library, the bookstore, and a handful of restaurants that weren't licensed to serve alcohol.

Tourists ventured to Mount Airy from all over the country, by the busload, to stroll down a handful of quaint blocks on North Main Street. They stopped by the famed Snappy Lunch restaurant to sample the town's signature pork-chop sandwich. They bought kitschy souvenirs in the gift shops. They talked about hometown-boy Andy Griffith and what America used to be like when times were simpler. Once, a friend visiting from New York City bought a can of soda at one of the mom-and-pop shops up the street. When the cashier told her how little it cost, she actually shrieked in disbelief. Mayberry really did exist!

That comforting sense of simplicity the tourists longed for was what I was there for, too. The best moments of my childhood had passed on summer visits with my cousins in a western Pennsylvania town about a quarter the size of Mount Airy. The adults, busy with work and unbearably long stretches of sitting on porches talking about who knows what, left us alone all day and all summer long in our private world of woods and sprawling back yards. If we needed to go anywhere—to the convenience store for junk food we wouldn't be allowed to eat at home or our grandmother's house for a Klondike bar—we walked a mile or two to get there. Around dinner time, somebody's mom would yell the hot dogs were grilled or we needed to take a shower for the first time in three days.

It was a carefree world, one in which enough order prevailed to keep us safe but not so much we couldn't freely explore its edges all day long. I didn't want to go to bed at night and couldn't wait to get up in the morning. All these years later, Mount Airy seemed like a chance to reclaim that magic. Indeed, the newspaper-bureau office, with its haze of smoke wafting over from the circulation manager's desk and the constant crackle of the police scanner, closely approximated evenings in my cousin's basement, where I lost games of RISK while my uncle smoked his second pack of the day and spread out wads of cash as he counted up his earnings from his convenience store and garage.

There was just one problem with life in Mayberry: I couldn't breathe.

The trouble started one chilly night in late January 1999, about a week before the move to Mount Airy. The afternoon had gone badly. I'd spent it down at the paper's head office in Winston-Salem, apologizing to a town manager for inadvertently publishing a map that suggested he planned to annex large portions of a neighboring town. The morning had been exhausting. It started with a lengthy drive to Mount Airy's Main Street barbershop, where an old-timer who'd served as the model for *The Andy Griffith Show*'s Floyd the barber was celebrating a birthday. Before I'd had a chance to consider how I would write about that, I jumped into a photographer's car and drove over the state line into Virginia, where a rock slide had closed a well-traveled thoroughfare. We followed a twisting back road until we came upon it. Tons upon tons of giant chunks of rock were strewn across both lanes, and a stench was rising from the animals trapped beneath. Nobody was driving past when it happened, which was a good thing because they would have been pulverized. We started knocking on doors to get quotes from neighbors, grabbed a late lunch in a smoky restaurant that gave me a wicked headache, and then headed back down to Winston-Salem, so I could start writing up both stories for my crusty, combative editor. By nighttime, I felt like I was on the bottom of the rock pile.

On the drive home in the dark that evening, my chest tightened. Sharp pains shot through it. My breathing turned shallow. I sweated despite the cold night. Within an hour I was slumped over the toilet, roiled by nausea and dizziness, my hands numb and tingling. Convinced I was having a heart attack, I nearly called 911. I hadn't exercised regularly in years, and nutrition for me meant alternating Krispy Kreme donuts with microwaveable Hungry-Man TV dinners.

But I was only twenty-six! How could my heart be bad already? I lay in bed that night, mostly awake, gasping for air at times, consumed with the certainty that something was terribly wrong. But when the doctor examined me the next morning, he couldn't find anything. He listened to my heart. It sounded fine. He ordered an EKG just to be sure. Those results were fine also. "I can't really explain it," he said, clearly baffled. "It might just be allergies and post-nasal drip messing with your stomach." All I knew, I told him, was that I felt like I was going to die. He sent me home with a stack of allergy meds and a nasal spray.

The meds didn't help. Pangs still shot through my chest all day long. Constantly convinced I was about to collapse, I avoided the middle of rooms, sticking close to walls in case a bout of unsteadiness overcame me. My brain churned ceaselessly, always anticipating trouble, worrying at nearly every instant about what would go wrong next. It became extremely difficult to do my job, partly because I continually feared having an attack in the middle of an interview or on a lonely road way out in the county, and partly because I couldn't focus long enough to plan an article in my head, let alone sit down and actually write one. Having a boss with a famously wild temper didn't help, nor did the fact that I saw my girlfriend, who lived an hour south, only on weekends. Winter turned to spring and the chest pains and labored breathing persisted. Black thoughts began creeping into my head, as did sleepless nights spent sweating in bed, haunted by the fear of dying there alone.

◦◦◦

All of this was a long way from where I had been just two years earlier as a journalism intern in Washington, DC, with plenty of friends and what felt like purpose and direction. Back then, I'd work hard all day downtown making calls, visiting sources, and writing articles, then meet up with friends at quitting time. In the winter, we might linger in bookstores, surveying the magazine racks and tables of new releases, imagining the volumes we'd one day write. In the spring, we'd have a couple beers at a sidewalk café and then stroll to Georgetown or Dupont Circle for dinner, chattering the whole time about our goals and glittering prospects, like we were newspaperman Jake Barnes slumming around 1920s Paris in Hemingway's *The Sun Also Rises*, except we felt certain our endings would be happier.

Desperate to recover that sense of possibility, I made plans to visit my old friends in Washington. In bed the night before leaving, I sweated and tossed and kept getting up to fiddle with the air conditioning. Sleep was out of the question. Breathing normally was difficult. I hit the road the next morning with barely anything left in the tank. The trip, a five-hour crawl on jam-packed interstates, took what little was left. Several times I pulled off the road simply to calm my churning stomach. I subsisted that morning and afternoon on nothing but a bottle of Coke and two chicken nuggets, gagged down on the beltway outside Washington.

What should have been a fun dinner that night with a good friend in the humming heart of DC became an ordeal. My hands shook, I could barely sit still, and I feared falling down if I stood up. I tried to downplay it, but my friend Courtney knew something was wrong. I told her the doctor didn't have an answer. She didn't either, but she gave me a good piece of advice: stop drinking caffeine. And one more thing: see a different doctor. When I did just that a few weeks later back in Mount Airy, he finally confirmed I'd been suffering for several months—and probably a lot longer than that—from a fairly severe anxiety disorder.

It was a rather mysterious condition. Symptoms could come and go quite suddenly or stick around for a very long time. There was no consensus on what caused the disorder or the best way to treat it. This much was certain, however: not a single symptom eluded me. Shortness of breath, heart palpitations, trembling and shaking. Check. Sweating, choking, nausea. Check. Dizziness and unsteadiness. Double check. Feelings of detachment, chills, fear of dying, fear of going crazy. Absolutely. Some experts stressed medication as the answer. Others favored changes in diet. Relaxation techniques, therapy, journal writing, and exercise were all recommended. I had nothing to lose by trying all of them.

And so began a new routine of plodding slowly around the block three times a week in my jogging shoes. It offered some relief from the stress and plenty of time to ponder my troubles and, even more, how I'd wandered so far into the wilderness in the first place. When had these problems really started? And why? Finding these answers mattered deeply to me, not merely because of a natural desire for order and reason, but also because they offered hope that my illness wasn't just randomly genetic and possibly incurable.

I desperately wanted to know it had started at a particular time for understandable reasons that could be unearthed, examined, and hopefully addressed. The truth, I realized, wouldn't reveal itself quite so neatly in all likelihood. But in digging into this issue like the intrepid reporter I was, it made sense to begin with hard questions about times I would mostly rather forget. And that made high school a logical starting point.

"With the exception of those privileged souls who under-stood right from the beginning what the problem really was, and who immediately set out upon the true, rough road of spiritual childhood and humility, the greater part of humankind is called upon to undergo a hard and painful experience," spiritual-master Carlo Carretto writes.[1] These hardships, these wilderness years, are the rule rather than the exception, and they befall us, Carretto says, because we can't mature properly without them. They come in phases, whipsawing us from exhilaration to panic and hope to complacency. They can arrive at any time in our lives. Often, Carretto says, it's around the age of forty. All that separates one wilderness experience from another is the details—and what we try to make of them.

That time in the wilderness was necessary and unavoid-able shouldn't have come as a surprise to me. Indeed, the stories I so enjoyed reading from a well-worn, illustrated children's bible made this point clear: most of us take our first, halting steps toward a calling way out in the fearsome wild. The Hebrews wandered there for years. David slung stones at Goliath in the badlands. John the Baptist brought forth from the wild the Good News. Jesus himself tangled with the devil in the wilderness before beginning his public ministry. The vocations these figures grew into would be unimaginable without the wilderness in which they were rooted, where the threat of oblivion always loomed along-side the promise of renewal and new beginnings. Whether it's a place on the map or a struggle in our minds, it's the wilderness that tests us and molds us. It can feel like its very intent is to break us down, making plain the problem of our stubborn pride and self-reliance, toughening us up for the long journey of vocation.

In my case, that journey began in my hometown of York, Pennsylvania, in the fall of 1989. I was a typical sixteen-year-old kid who'd been attending Mass and Sunday school for a good ten years, saying my prayers when I really wanted something. Of course I knew the biblical stories of trials in uncharted lands. But to me they were just old stories. I never guessed that the wilds could creep up so close to a well-manicured suburban neighborhood, right into my second-floor bedroom, straight into my head. That was about to change.

Early in my junior year of high school, a good friend who was rather dismayed by my devotion to the sports page and thin newsweeklies (and my relative neglect of more serious subject matter) took it upon himself to turn me on to real literature. My teachers had been trying in vain to do the same for several years. At that time, every subject at school was the same to me—technical material that needed to be mastered and converted into the *A* grades that brought admission to an elite college. Academic performance was my one and only measure of success. But things changed one day after school when my friend drove me over to the Bookland store on Edgar Street. I started off hunting for a "classic" that I could swiftly review and check off the list for my next assignment in the English class we were in together. I'd just completed a rather hysterical term paper on the many virtues of the death penalty and was now dreaming of being a prosecutor—so *Crime and Punishment*, described on its back cover as "a story of a murder and its consequences," immediately caught my eye.[2]

The novel, initially to my dismay, turned out to be about much more than a loser who deserved beheading. Raskolnikov, a former student living aimlessly and destitute in St. Petersburg, kills a pawnbroker and her sister in an attempt to steal some money and improve his condition. Detectives suspect him right away, touching off an inner drama in which he agonizes over what to do as police close in. Ultimately, he confesses and heads to prison in Siberia, where he tries to build a new life grounded in an emerging sense of faith and love. The notions explored in the book—ambition, suffering, hubris, and honor, to name a few—offered a powerful glimpse of how complex life really could be and how embarrassingly little I actually knew about it. I'd taken a big bite from the apple, and the sweet sensation of new worlds opening up was electrifying.

Many books followed, often at the expense of the ones I was supposed to be studying for school—Steinbeck, Fitzgerald, T. S. Eliot, Hemingway, Samuel Beckett, and Joseph Conrad, to name a few. But no one turned me on quite like French existentialist Albert Camus. "No, please not Camus!" my younger brother Jeff pleads even to this day, recalling the drama that unfolded in our house as I steeped myself in the angst of *The Stranger*.

Certainly, this newfound literary sense made me a more independent thinker. After years of seeing education as an exercise in gamely playing the system, I started questioning everything, and it didn't take long to train my sights on the Church. Mercifully, the details of how this rather predictable rebellion played out are rather fuzzy now. But the gist of it was this: the more I thought about religious faith—and in my mother's large Italian family it was the most fundamental of all realities—the more absurd it all seemed. Nietzsche said it was for weaklings; Marx called it the opiate of the masses—and I sure as heck was neither of those. Where was the evidence of God's existence? If God did exist, why was there so much injustice in the world? Why, for example, was I still lacking a girlfriend when I clearly deserved one?

I began to make caustic remarks about religion in school and around my family. I took pride in no longer saying "under God" during the Pledge of Allegiance. My mother, though of the more mild "northern" Italian persuasion, had seen enough. "What *do* you believe?" she hollered in frustration one afternoon as I ranted about the idiocy of the faithful. Dashing upstairs, I grabbed my copy of *The Stranger*, stormed back into the kitchen, and declared, "This is what I believe!" By the end of high school, I was no longer going to Mass—and this new sense of freedom, a hallmark of early days in the wilderness, was exhilarating.

The thrill hadn't lasted more than six months, however, before I recognized the dead end toward which my flirtation with Camus was heading. I'm a practical guy prone to following ideas to their logical conclusion, and the conclusion here was pretty stark: if God didn't exist, then life was in fact entirely meaningless. Camus seemed okay with that. Then again, he'd been a handsome, famous, supremely gifted hero of the French Resistance who never suffered for female companionship. He'd had enough distractions, I supposed, that he could stay content by simply enjoying the finer things in life until it all ended, quite suddenly and prematurely in his case. That, to say the least, was not my situation, and the existentialist stance on life—the notion that we can create our own meaning in an absurd world by living authentically—never warmed me.

Despite being one of the top students in my class, despite the near constant praise from teachers, despite a close group of friends and a future that everyone believed was very bright, I felt increasingly tormented—unhappy with my looks, my abilities, and my social graces. I thoroughly disliked myself, and letting go of my faith, as unsophisticated as it had been, left me completely rudderless. Most of the time, I kept despair at bay through sheer busyness. But when something went badly wrong—and by that I mean a failed romantic relationship, of which there were a few—despair stretched out inside me like a great cave. I'd plunge into a depression of sorts that at first lasted for several days and later could stretch on for weeks. I was, without even realizing it, way out into the wilderness.

Even my arrival at Duke proved disappointing. My freshman year should have been a crowning moment, considering how I'd single-mindedly plotted all through high school to get into a college like it. Instead, the bottom fell out. Being surrounded by hundreds of classmates who were at least as smart as I was and, in many cases, more sophisticated, better looking, more athletic, and more popular was challenging in itself. Still, the first semester had been marked by excellent grades and a blossoming friendship with a fun, affectionate woman who seemed interested in something more than friendship. And though I wanted that relationship to work more than I'd ever wanted anything, my own self-doubts poisoned it fairly badly.

We started off the second semester with some painful conversations about what we were looking for in the relationship and the ways in which it wasn't working. Our talks were intense and honest and ended the way these things often do, with great awkwardness. Though in later years we were to become good friends again, we ended up not speaking for the rest of that school year. I felt a hollowness that far surpassed anything I'd experienced, and it lasted the whole winter and well into the spring. And it wasn't even really about the girl. It had far more to do with my longstanding dislike of myself and an inability to ignore it any longer—or see a way out of it.

One sunny, wind-swept winter morning, I was trudging along Markham Avenue in Durham. Across the street at Asbury Methodist Church, Sunday services were just letting out. Churchgoers stood outside in little groups, chatting and laughing, full of good cheer, in stark contrast to my exhaustion, aimlessness, and deep sadness. From where I stood, it looked like their lives were informed by a sense of purpose and meaning that mine sorely lacked. They gathered regularly among a community of friends, and they prayed to a God they believed in and who armored them for whatever challenges came their way. Most of all, they had, I suspected, a clear notion of how they fit into the world and what was required of them. How I longed for the same knowledge. How impossible it seemed that I would ever find it.

Looking back, I can see now that, like Dante, I needed a "Virgil" to guide me out of the dark woods, out of the maze of my own misconceptions. I found such a person at Duke: a professor named Wallace Fowlie. Friends at school kept bringing his name up, talking about an amazing course he taught, fittingly, on Dante's *Inferno*.

Fowlie was an older guy, so old that he'd been a student of T. S. Eliot at Harvard in the 1930s. He'd been close friends with the novelist Henry Miller, and he'd written several acclaimed books about French poets and novelists. He'd done a groundbreaking translation of Arthur Rimbaud's complete works. Rock-legend Jim Morrison of the Doors had read it and even sent Fowlie a thank-you note saying he carried the book wherever he went. I missed the cutoff for Fowlie's Dante course, but I made sure to enroll in his class on Marcel Proust's *Remembrance of Things Past* in the spring of my sophomore year. There was no way I was going to miss out on a guy who'd merited a note from the Lizard King, as Morrison had labeled himself. And Fowlie was every bit as good as advertised—unremarkably short, stocky, and bald but mesmerizing with his baritone voice. He was even at work on a book comparing the poetry of Rimbaud and Morrison, whose music he enjoyed but whose talent he kept in perspective. ("It's a book about a great poet and a much lesser one," he once told me.)

Halfway through the semester, a group of us went to dinner with him and then back to his small apartment in Chapel Hill, where we bombarded him with questions. I was standing in the dim light, half-listening to his answers, more entranced by his giant poster on the wall of a leather-clad Jim Morrison, when I heard him say, "Well, of course, I'm Catholic." Had I heard that correctly? Here was a man who'd personally befriended a virtual literary hall of fame—from Eliot to Robert Penn Warren—a man whose learning and sophistication far exceeded that of anyone I'd ever met, and he was saying, quite matter of factly, that he was Catholic, and that he embraced all the rewards, demands, joys, sorrows, and bafflements that came with that commitment.

Fowlie and I grew close over the next several years. He became a spiritual mentor and sage and a personal conduit into a world of writers who'd previously existed to me only as icons on a bookshelf. After several years of stumbling about in the wilderness, despairing and disconsolate, I felt a new and welcome emotion: hope. It's not that I was blind to Fowlie's flaws—occasional defensiveness and considerable pride among them. He was simply an extraordinary man—so learned, so perceptive, and so capable, despite his age and stature, of connecting with students more than sixty years his junior. And all of it was grounded in his Catholic faith, which, as it turned out, was his single greatest priority.

Fowlie showed me something I hadn't fully believed— that faith and learning could intersect at a very high plane. A chapter in Fowlie's memoir, *Aubade,* explored his evolution from Baptist to Episcopalian to Catholic, and I read it over and over again. I noted in particular the long history of the Church and its traditions and saints made a powerful impression on Fowlie. Spending my junior year of college in England, I came to see what he meant. Visiting churches in France, Italy, Austria, and elsewhere provided noble reasons for cutting class. It also made the ancient roots of Catholicism more vivid and meaningful. On one memorable afternoon, I rode a bus from Nice into the town of Vence, home of Matisse's Chapelle du Rosaire, which Fowlie greatly admired. Its spare design, clean lines, bold colors, and sudden, startling plays of light stood in stark contrast to my own cluttered, half-lit basement of doubt, heaviness, and dog-eared Camus novels.

Couldn't I embrace a simpler, more vibrant faith? Couldn't prayer feel the way this tiny chapel looked— vivid, focused, stripped down to an absolute essence in which not even a square inch of space is wasted? Back at

Duke as a senior, I took a fascinating survey of Catholicism with Bill Cavanaugh, then a doctoral student and
now a noted scholar at DePaul University. Bill brought the
counter-cultural dimensions of Catholicism alive for us,
contrasting the rather bland, suburban faith in which I'd
grown up with the hard-edged, uncompromising, social-
justice-driven lives of Oscar Romero and Dorothy Day. One
afternoon, John Dear, a Duke graduate and controversial
Jesuit priest who'd served prison time for his protest at a
US Air Force base, stopped by for a visit to Cavanaugh's
class. The powerful intellectual dimensions of Catholicism,
of which I'd been mostly unaware, startled me with their
power, logic, and passion.

The Catholic student group at Duke made regular
retreats to Mepkin Abbey, a Trappist monastery in the lowlands of South Carolina. I wasn't a member of the group,
but a friend who was raved about the place. Also, a literature professor I had that semester had written a favorable
piece for a national magazine about his visit there. Even
without their encouragement, I'd by now read enough
Thomas Merton to want to go behind a monastery's walls
myself. Besides, who else among my friends would be taking a spring-break trip like this?

Jim Morrison might have sang about breaking through,
but it seemed to me upon arriving for a long weekend
that these monks were really doing it. And as far as I
could tell, knowing that one was really alive had nothing
to do with the mind-altering drugs that led Morrison to
his early grave. The monks' lives were much more about
self-abnegation than self-indulgence. They devoted themselves to a relentless schedule of worship, study, and work,
rising every day at 3:00 a.m. for their first prayers of the

day. Never before had I seen St. Paul's injunction to pray without ceasing lived out so completely. The mindfulness, the grit, and the humility of the monks made a lasting impression; prayer was in fact a vocation in itself, probably the highest of all vocations—and I knew virtually nothing about it!

By the time graduation rolled around, I was once again a regular at Sunday Mass, and I was determined to make up for lost time. After several years of spiritual wandering and intense struggle with my own sense of self-worth, it felt hugely liberating to adopt what I thought was a more mature faith on my own terms. After all of the uncertainty and ambiguity, I wanted clear-cut answers that required actual implementation.

So, fresh out of college, I took a one-year job on Duke's campus as an editorial assistant at a science journal. It wasn't the most obvious way to use an English degree, but it at least disproved my premed and engineering friends who doubted it could be used at all. I figured this gig would give me time to sort out the real nature of my vocation, which remained murky, beyond a vague sense of wanting to read, write, grow in my faith, find meaningful work, and, at some point, raise a family. I'd seen the power of calling in people like Wallace Fowlie and Bill Cavanaugh and wanted that same sense of purpose for myself. And hanging around Duke would help me stay connected with the local faith community while I got serious about living out the catechism to the letter.

◦⟲◦

There's a reason the world is not over-populated with Mother Teresas. Living a virtuous life on any terms, especially Catholic ones, is in itself a journey into the wild. As I began to embrace my childhood faith as an adult, the inevitable questions that all young-adult Catholics wrestle with began to arise. Some of the Vatican's stances were puzzling to me, and they made even less sense to my Baptist girlfriend.

By now, I'd read a good bit of Thomas Merton, including his book *New Seeds of Contemplation*. In it he says: "The man who does not permit his spirit to be beaten down and upset by dryness and helplessness, but who lets God lead him peacefully through the wilderness, and desires no other support or guidance than that of pure faith and trust in God alone, will be brought to the Promised Land."[3] I didn't underline that passage then, as I often did in blue pen when encountering sage advice. This is probably due to the fact that, despite my return to the Catholic faith, deep down I had no intention of being "led" anywhere. As I saw it at the time, I'd made it this far out of the valley of doubt largely through my own efforts, and I planned to hack through the rest of the brush on my own. I soldiered on, determined to uphold the spiritual and social teachings of the Church—and eager to cast a condescending eye toward anyone who didn't.

I started volunteering as a tutor for a local adult-literacy program. I never missed a Mass. I fasted when required and showed up for holy days of obligation. It seemed I was making all the right moves. Rather than bringing me greater peace, however, these efforts gradually stoked real anger and resentment—at my girlfriend for questioning what I was trying to do, at acquaintances and friends who thought I'd gone a little batty with my post-Camus enthusiasms, and at people in general, especially students at Duke who were having a grand time living a life of pleasure that now felt entirely inaccessible to me.

Doubts inevitably emerged. Hadn't Merton and Day both lived bohemian lives when they were my age? What about St. Augustine? He was the one who said, "Give me chastity, but not yet," for crying out loud. They all had their wilderness years. What the heck was I doing trying to build an orderly city of virtue at twenty-two?

Merton was right, though I couldn't see it then. We can't lead ourselves out of the wilderness through sheer force of will. There are times when we're obviously mired in it. There are other times when it feels like we've returned to civilization, only to find it's just the terrain that's changed. We don't need a strategy for making it out of the wild. We can't even create one. We just need to stay on our feet as much as we can and trust. I didn't know this at the time, however. My one-year stint at the science journal was ending, and, though I'd spent countless hours philosophizing in my own journal, where I'd theoretically evaluated and rejected at least six different career paths, I wasn't any closer to a real calling.

My girlfriend, having been exceptionally patient and accepting of my quirks, finally called out the obvious: our two-year relationship was collapsing under the weight of my frustration and her own restlessness. She made plans to attend law school in California. Other friends were getting on with their lives too—in medical school, graduate school, or in full-time jobs that actually provided health insurance. The hope that had surged through me during the second half of college had been a soul-saving gift. But I'd failed to nurture it with any real exploration of my desires or dedicated focus that would have improved my health and productivity. That's a fancy way of stating the blunt truth: I was still too immature and self-centered to take seriously the demands and possibilities that faith afforded. As it easily can in the wilderness, hope had succumbed to a false sense of self-reliance, which in turn succumbed to complacency.

On the strength of a few freelance journalism projects I'd done at Duke, I hastily applied for and rather miraculously received an internship with a magazine in Washington, DC. There I spent four months fact-checking stories about young politicos and outrageous private-school tuition fees. It was an exciting place, surrounded as I was by staffers deep into their book projects or showing up for spots on CNN. When that internship ended, I took another one at a weekly newspaper covering the higher-education industry. Suddenly, I was routinely covering congressional hearings, writing articles every week, and learning a craft under the constant pressure of deadlines and smart, demanding editors.

It was always a thrill to stride out the front door of the office onto Twenty-Fourth Street, hail a cab, and tell the driver, "Capitol Hill, please." After previous stints as a newspaper carrier, grocery-store clerk, and AAA travel consultant who never quite got the hang of transferring tags and titles, I'd finally found engaging work. With no family or girlfriend or any other obligations to speak of, work was pretty much all I wanted to do and, in fact, all I did. Faith remained a priority *in theory*. But I was away from Durham, and my Catholic friends and gradually started missing Sunday Masses here and there. Books on journalism became more appealing than volumes about saints. One afternoon a colleague walked into the office with a big smudge on his head. On the verge of alerting him, I realized I'd forgotten all about Ash Wednesday.

My internship ended, and, having been advised by several mentors to get some newspaper training, I headed back to North Carolina as an education reporter at a daily in the town of High Point. The plan was to put in a little time there and then get back up to DC and into a better job as fast as possible. It wasn't easy work. The editor demanded each reporter write at least forty articles a month. That equated to about two stories a day and some pretty awful journalism all around. "NBA draft crap," the paper once announced in a headline, instead of the intended "NBA draft crop." Another time an editor sent around a message saying there was a birthday cake at his desk "in honor of moi." A colleague a few feet away looked up and said, in all seriousness, "Who's Moey?"

Still, I was hell-bent on succeeding in my new profession and put in whatever time it took. That usually meant lingering at dreadfully dull school-board meetings, racing back to the office to file on deadline around 11:00 p.m., and then watching television on the floor of my nearly furnitureless apartment as I wolfed down a frozen fried-chicken entrée at midnight.

_◊_

There are many ways to lose ourselves in the wilderness. You can do it spectacularly and publicly, like Nicolas Cage's dying alcoholic in *Leaving Las Vegas*, stumbling around escalators and wrecking poolside furniture. Or it can happen with no fanfare at all, so quietly that even you don't notice the crackling of the leaves as you stray off the path.

My single-mindedness at work earned me an entry-level job with a bigger newspaper in Winston-Salem, where I was at the very bottom of the food chain. Any chance of getting promoted to a second-tier bureau office (like the one I would eventually get to in Mount Airy) meant showing, in my mind at least, there was nothing more important than my job. Everything else fell away as I worked constantly to scratch out stories in boring bedroom communities where news was rarely committed. I volunteered for extra assignments and tried desperately, as I always had, to please everyone all the time. It was a day-to-day existence lived almost entirely in my head, where a tape of the important changes I planned to make ran constantly— things like working out, reacquainting myself with vegetables, or visiting Dr. Fowlie. Long hours lost to stunningly boring town-council and planning-board meetings left me baffled and increasingly frustrated. What connection did all this blather about property setbacks and hundred-year flood plans have with finding a calling? On some level, I must have known the bill was coming due.

Late one night in August 1998, I walked into my apartment. The new-message light flashed on my answering machine. "Hi, Stephen," I heard my mom say. "I just saw in the paper—and you probably already know this—that Dr. Fowlie died a few days ago. I was sorry to see that." In fact, I hadn't known he'd died. I hadn't even been in touch with him for a year. Several times I'd nearly picked up the phone to say hello, but, having heard his health wasn't great, figured I'd try again soon. He was nearly ninety after all; of course, he'd have his down days.

The message clicked off, and my heart started to race, and my stomach dropped, the way it did sometimes when I was writing on deadline and time was running out—except those things always got fixed. And instinctively I was scheming about how to fix this, too, that maybe if I played that message a second time I wouldn't hear what I thought I'd heard and wouldn't have to accept what haunted me instantly and always will—that a man who'd changed my life, whose friendship and influence had been indescribable in its power, had died in a hospital room in Durham, and I'd been too wrapped up in my own head and meager little world to share even the briefest of good-byes.

It would be a few months before I moved to Mount Airy and the panic attacks started, but I was already lost again in that dark wood, far deeper than before, and my guide was gone.

CHAPTER TWO

Awareness: Creating a Call on the Fly

WHEN YOU HEAR COACHES TALK ABOUT THE NCAA basketball tournament, their strategy is nearly always the same: survive and advance. Don't worry about the next game, just focus on the entirely unpredictable one in front of you right now. That's how I spent that summer of 1999, surviving and advancing through each second. Every day began and ended with a pill meant to ease the anxiety symptoms.

Many years later, I'm still unclear on whether the pills actually helped. They definitely did something—within thirty minutes of swallowing the pill, my whole body overheated, my ears hummed, and my head, for an hour or two, felt detached from the rest of my body. Still, it was hard to picture myself worse off than I was already, so I kept on taking them.

I showered regularly but only bothered shaving occasionally, and that made the morning routine pretty easy. I'd walk out the front door of my house and across the street to the office amid the convicts and parolees, my head buzz-ing in a medicine-induced haze. Then, knees flexing, arms swinging as if they belonged to someone else, up the steps of the grand post office I would go to retrieve the morn-ing's mail—mostly smaller, competing newspapers from which I'd swipe the most promising story ideas and rere-port them myself. Some days I traveled the lonely, twisting roads of Surry and Stokes counties in search of a story. There was one about a young couple who chose to spend their honeymoon in Andy Griffith's boyhood home, which was now available for rental. There was another on a shoot-out at a nearby farm between a father and son, profiled on *America's Most Wanted*, and what appeared to be about half of the cops in North Carolina. Other days I propped my feet on the desk and read from Arthur Schlesinger's mas-sive biography of Robert F. Kennedy.

Around noon, I'd grab a *Sports Illustrated* and a vial of Xanax and trudge up Main Street to a favorite lunch coun-ter, weaving among the tourists, steering clear of pork-chop sandwiches. The afternoons dragged by in similar fashion. Survive and advance. Around six, I walked back across the street, changed out of my standard journalist uniform of frayed khakis and a faded dress shirt from Sears, and laced up my running shoes. I'd chug along at a modest trot, heading south on Main Street, making a right on West Wilson and then a left on Spring, all the way up to the elementary school. Then it was back down the length of the modest homes on Spring, around the corner onto Church Street, and back to my house. Maybe two miles total. I never timed my pace. There was only one objective: finishing the run without stopping to walk a single step.

It was, I realize now, a metaphor for the entire summer—the art of putting one foot in front of the other
again and again, especially when it felt the least possible.
Even this modest endeavor, coupled with the surprisingly hot foothill afternoons, proved exhausting, leaving
me hunched over on the front steps of the house, heav-
ing and drenched. Still, I rather enjoyed it. As I sweated
and groaned through the early evening, I envisioned the
heat and the strain frying the anxiety inside my head and
my heart, like a fever cooking a pesky virus. Sometimes
I addressed the anxiety directly. "How do you like this,
you jerk?" I'd say aloud, hauling myself up a hill. "You're
gonna be sorry you messed with me." And so it went deep
into the shimmering summer.

⟡

The wilderness is vast, so big that it's easy to forget it's
just the first stage on our journey of vocation. Most of
us languish there for a time, and it's only fitting that we
do. If John the Baptist and Jesus Christ paid their dues in
uncharted lands, should we really expect an easier road for
ourselves? Eventually, though, we need to find our bear-
ings, gather what we've learned, and head back, as they
did, to civilization. To do that, we need awareness—and
we reach it by working with God to take a hard look at
ourselves.

Awareness doesn't solve our challenges, but it does
grant us the perspective to see them in new ways, to see
ourselves in new ways, too, and to start imagining new
possibilities. We begin to recognize, perhaps for the first
time, our strengths and weaknesses and size up who we
really are. If time in the wilderness provides us a vast

wealth of experience both pleasant and painful, awareness helps us make sense of it. It starts molding our raw living into practical knowledge. It's a state we can't force ourselves into; it builds slowly through tiny moments, choices, and accidents.

For Fr. James Martin, S.J., the Jesuit priest and best-selling author, awareness started with a television show. Returning to his apartment one evening after another numbing day as a fast-track executive at General Electric, Martin happened upon a documentary of the famed Trappist monk, Thomas Merton. Martin wasn't particularly religious and had never heard of Merton. But this account of how a man found deep meaning through a life of prayer, service, and writing, instead of the endless pursuit of money and the next promotion, gripped Martin. That moment prompted him to read *The Seven Storey Mountain*, Merton's classic autobiographical account of his religious conversion. Sensing he was onto something big, Martin read more of Merton's work. Huddled one night over *No Man Is an Island* after another lousy day in the office, Martin came across this passage:

> Why do we have to spend our lives striving to be something we would never want to be, if we only knew what we wanted? Why do we waste our time doing things which, if we only stopped to think about them, are just the opposite of what we were made for?[1]

Answering those questions ultimately led Martin to the priesthood, where he has found deep meaning and purpose. He only arrived at that happy destination, however, because he first embraced the challenge of looking unhappiness in the eye. It would have been easy enough for Martin to shrug off his misgivings and discontent as a phase, or merely the product of being in the wrong job in the wrong organization. He might have easily settled for many more well-compensated, prestigious, miserable years in the corporate trenches.

It's much harder to stop in midstride and question the very fundamentals on which our lives are built. But Martin did it anyway, baffling his family and friends by walking away from everything he'd worked for to start over. That can be what it takes, though, to create lasting awareness, to edge toward what we're made for. As Martin found, God does send us the help we need to become more aware. But quite often it does not arrive the way we would prefer. It comes by way of serious challenges out in the wilderness that harshly test our limits.

Certainly anxiety constituted that kind of challenge for me. For about ten years, without even knowing it, I'd battled a low-grade version of the illness, which often left me angry, defensive, and worried for reasons I couldn't understand or explain. Like Martin toiling away at GE, I submerged my troubles for as long as I could, avoiding a deep, scary dive into my soul and letting a vague hope of change carry me along instead. I lived in denial until the last possible moment. Wracked for months by chest pains, dizziness, and despair, I nevertheless went without any treatment at all, hoping desperately that the problems would resolve themselves. Even sitting in the doctor's office, with all the tests ruling out anything but a substantial issue with anxiety, I initially dismissed his efforts to prescribe medication.

The crisis point finally came the week leading up to the Fourth of July. I'd just returned to Mount Airy from

Pennsylvania, where my dad was recovering from a dicey operation for prostate cancer. Seeing him, a guy always crackling with energy, stretched feebly out on a bed in his den, ratcheted my anxiety symptoms to new levels. Within days, I could barely drive and couldn't eat more than a few bites of food without retching. By the time I made it back to Mount Airy, I was coming undone. My apartment's window-unit air conditioner didn't make a dent in the midsummer heat wave. A couple days after my return home, it quit working altogether. I called my landlord from the sweltering apartment to report that the unit was broken and dripping water onto the floor. "The hardwoods!" he yelped. "It'll ruin the hardwoods!" Meanwhile, I found it almost impossible to rest at night. And that was how I spent the week—gagging down bites of chicken here and there, sleeping maybe an hour or two each night, and banging out articles by day in the office.

One day that week I went out to report on a new section of interstate highway that was about to open. Parking near a still-unopened exit ramp, I got out of the car to look for someone from the construction crew to interview. Nobody was around. So I hiked through some tall grass up an incline for a better view. I still couldn't spot anyone. But looking down, I was horrified to find my belt, pants, and shoes crawling with ticks. In my state of pure exhaustion, they appeared three times their size. Each of them, I was convinced, was about to infect me with a dreaded disease. It was the most surreal week of my life, maddening, unrelenting, and unsustainable. On Friday evening, I filed my last story of the week, slumped into my Corolla, and drove an hour south to visit my girlfriend, Dawn, a fellow journalist whom I'd started dating the year before. The whole way down, the hills on both sides of the road seemed to close on my head like a vice. I'd barely taken a step into Dawn's condo before breaking down completely.

And that is how my pride was broken too. I'd reached the absolute end of what I could do on my own—and realized how woefully short I was on answers to my troubles. Though I was too distraught to grasp it at the time, I was, in this pathetic state, finally learning something about dependence on God. The monks at Mepkin, where I'd visited a couple more times since college, stressed the importance of receptivity, a state of openness to God's action in our lives. It was a quality they spent decades developing, so I clearly hadn't acquired it over the course of six or seven months. At least, however, it was a concept no longer merely cataloged in my head but, finally, slowly taking root in my heart.

Those first movements of receptivity, I believe, marked the beginning of awareness. They were born of an ordeal, but, even in my badly addled state, there was a small part of me that knew this meant something. Because now, finally having to acknowledge that my long-established way of being no longer worked, I could start over, one fearful breath at a time. It was like crawling out of bed after an extended bout of nausea, a little wobbly and rather weak, every step requiring utmost caution.

The usual demons still lingered—dread of getting up in the morning, the enormous effort required to focus on writing even the simplest articles, the weird out-of-body sensations triggered by the medicine. Not sure exactly what to do next, I felt my way gingerly through the day. At night, I wrote in a journal, talked on the phone with Dawn, and read a wonderful book that I'd discovered in Mount Airy's

Main Street bookstore—*The Anxiety and Phobia Workbook* by Edmund J. Bourne. His urgent insistence that we make our physical and emotional well-being a top priority—and his detailed, practical suggestions for exactly how to do it—boosted my spirits and, more than that, made it increasingly clear that I needed to reorder my life. As I pondered what that meant, I kept on running.

One humid evening I'd finished my typical route and was walking a cool-down lap around the block, thinking, as always, about my situation. Somewhere on Spring Street came a simple, unexpected, elegant thought: "What if this anxiety isn't the enemy after all? What if it's really trying to help me?" It's true the past several months had been hell; I would have preferred to avoid them at any cost. It's also true my friends had predicted this would happen. One guy wrote in my high school yearbook that I lived too much inside my head; he expected it would eventually explode in a college library.

Changes were desperately needed. I was, of course, thinking about them, but I had not been making them. So my body and brain started to quit. Maybe they were sabotaging me. Or maybe they were telling me to change before it was too late. That sunny evening on Spring Street, amid the hum of air conditioners and the clink of dinner plates scraping against tables, there wasn't a flashing banner in the trees ahead suddenly announcing: "This Is the Most Important Day of Your Life!" And yet, I'm convinced it was. For in that instant my view of life and how to live it began to change, slowly but surely, and forever. Until then, I'd seen myself as a formerly healthy guy who was no longer well. From then on, I saw myself as a guy who'd been sick all his life and was finally getting better.

That moment, coming about a month after I hit rock bottom, offered proof that steep challenges aren't the only route by which God leads us toward awareness. He also favors us with sudden bolts of insight. He sends us grace. We have to be prepared to receive it, and our toughest challenge is to respond—to do that punishing work of saying yes, letting our willfulness be ground down until we're left with a choice—and to carry on as before, furiously denying the spiritual dependence and hunger that drives us, or, alternatively, welcoming our incompleteness and limitations with gratitude. We can continue to delude ourselves, perpetually occupied by distractions ranging from the unhelpful to the truly dangerous, or we can say with St. Paul, "Therefore, I am content with weaknesses, insults, hardships, persecutions, and constraints, for the sake of Christ; for when I am weak, then I am strong" (2 Cor 12:10).

Certainly I was weak in many ways. Following the advice in Bourne's book, I began taking stock of the different dimensions of my life, its physical, intellectual, emotional, and spiritual components. It wasn't surprising, upon reflection, that I'd fallen into this deep hole. Each area needed a lot of work, to say the least. As my adolescent friends had noticed, I'd lived for too long in my own head, ignoring my body and totally failing to see how my neglect of it might impact my brain.

The new running routine was helping turn the problem around, but I couldn't seriously call myself fit. Meanwhile, like many guys, my emotions were a territory mostly uncharted, and even when I could detect them, I didn't have the language to express them. Much work was required there. Intellect had always been my specialty, but gaps existed there too. Ten years of reading ambitiously and philosophizing endlessly created a lot of theoretical knowledge. Unfortunately, I had not yet read the book that explained how to apply it all to daily living. As far as faith went, I had good intentions—and that was about it. I had not attended church regularly or devoted myself to any regular spiritual practices for far too long.

Such was my assessment of myself. What was I going to do with it? I'd met a severe challenge and been reward-ed with some moments of sheer grace. It was here that I grasped a third stage of building awareness—taking responsibility. I'd concealed my illness from nearly every-one, relying on a small team that included Dawn, my brother, my doctor, a counselor, and a few trusted friends. They'd all provided crucial support. In the end, though, I was the only one who could do the full work of healing, and doing it wasn't easy. I was still plagued at times by chest pains and shortness of breath and, most of all, a fear of not being able to cope. I was also tired and more than a little bitter about my situation, my condition, and the toll these had taken. I saw many scapegoats, and even now, twelve years later, I can become startled at how much blame I'm still tempted to assign my bosses at the newspa-per, my landlord, Mayberry in general.

Still, I'd come too far to shortchange my recovery and was frankly frightened of what might happen if I didn't follow through. It was high time to hold myself account-able for my own future. Instinctively, I started drawing on the wisdom of the monks at Mepkin. Their example had been on my mind a great deal. During my most recent visit, about eighteen months before, I'd written a lengthy news-paper article about their way of life. When it came down to it, they made prayer, work, and study their top priorities.

They also kept things as simple as possible. Without ever quite committing to it in a conscious, highly deliberate way, I began to follow their approach. I knew enough now not to romanticize the lives of monks, which were, in some respects, far more demanding than most. But I kept coming back to the fact that, on the whole, the monks seemed focused and balanced. I was neither of those things.

My most immediate problem, looking at it from a monastic lens, was work. Monks needed it to make a living, whether it was raising chickens or baking bread or making jam. But they also saw work as more than making a living. By providing high-quality goods to people who needed them, they were also participating in God's creation, exchanging honest labor for a fair price. As much as I tried, I just couldn't find a similar level of meaning in my job. My boss was, by any standard, mercurial. I felt isolated in the small bureau office. And to be honest, I just wasn't very good at spinning the complicated web of relationships that small-town reporting required.

Living an hour away from Dawn, with whom I was growing increasingly close and whom I had only gotten to see on weekends for much of the past year, had also grown frustrating. I already knew my way around Greensboro, which she lived near, and had some friends there. In this case, being in a bigger city would actually make my life easier. So, when an offer to cover business for the Greensboro daily newspaper came through near the end of the summer, I accepted right away. On a bright Saturday morning in late August 1999, Dawn and Ken, the chain-smoking circulation manager I shared my office with, helped shovel my beloved futon and several boxes of books and ratty clothes into a U-Haul heading out of Mayberry. I'd arrived in town in a flurry of naïveté and ambition, focused 100 percent on my job and career prospects, convinced I'd found my calling. I left having learned, as any monk would have told me, that a job is often just a fraction of a calling. Having now survived the most intense anxiety-stricken months, I no longer had any overarching ambitions. It seemed my vocation, for the time being at least, was simply to enjoy my days as much as possible and be grateful for that, instead of merely staggering through them in a cloud of panic and fear. I approached my new job in Greensboro with the seriousness of a guy who wanted to make the most of what felt like a second chance. I tried hard, however, not to lose sight of the fact that other aspects of my life needed tending as well.

There was, for instance, the matter of prayer. It was the pinnacle of the monastic way and yet had somehow devolved into an afterthought for me. I hadn't attended Mass regularly for three years. Even now, it's not entirely clear why. Perhaps I needed some distance from the false religious certainty of my college years, which bred smugness, which in turn bred dissatisfaction, which later helped cause a breakdown. Perhaps the strain of dealing with the anxiety at its peak left no room for prayer. (Though very late one Saturday night in Mayberry I'd picked up the phone and called the local Catholic church for a listing of the next day's Masses. Expecting a recording, I instead got the parish priest himself, snapped out of sleep and none too happy about it. He chewed me out and hung up.)

Certainly, thoughts of God were never that far from my mind. I'd find my way to church on occasion and pick up a book of spiritual reflections now and then. Even during my bleakest moments of the previous year, I'd never felt abandoned by God or resentful toward him. Indeed, those fleeting moments of grace, though not fully comprehended at the time, suggested he was aware of my crisis and was helping me through it. Getting back to church and a more active spiritual life was really about making room for it, the same way I had for exercise and a better diet. But I wasn't making that space—so Dawn did instead.

Dawn, who'd grown up as an on-again, off-again Presbyterian, was a reporter who didn't mind asking blunt questions. Accustomed to the stacks of books in my apartment with titles like *Mere Christianity* and *Life and Holiness* and also as the prime recipient of my many spiritual-philosophical musings, she posed this zinger: "You keep talking and reading about God and faith and why it's so important. Why don't you start going to church? Why don't we start going together?" It was the swift kick in the pants that I needed.

The very next week Dawn accompanied me to Mass. She liked it, and so did I. We kept going for the rest of the summer of 2000, and it quickly became part of our routine. Two years later we were married in the Church. At our home parish, I got involved with the church's communications ministry, and Dawn started the process of converting to Catholicism. Serving as her sponsor required attending a lot of classes, which reconnected me to the faith of my youth. As adults, though, the stakes were higher for all of us. Seeing the transformative effect the conversion experience had on her and many other members of her class (almost all of whom were older than we were, and making significant sacrifices to join the Church), made a powerful impression. One of the leaders of the class referred me to a spiritual director, who offered valuable guidance and

introduced me to forms of contemplative prayer. For the
first time, my spirtual life was becoming multifaceted. No
longer content just to read an occasional book about prayer,
I was more deeply engaged in its actual practice.

And true to the monastic formula for success, engage-
ment with prayer increased my desire to study it. With the
same fervor in which I had immersed myself in Camus and
his existentialist peers back in high school, I now explored
the work of spiritual masters. In particular, given that I
wasn't going to be a monk myself and needed to exist in
the nine-to-five world, I relentlessly sought wisdom about
how to incorporate faith into everyday life, where the
hurly-burly of merely getting along makes it tough to keep
our eyes cast toward heaven. Shipments of books arrived at
our condo routinely, bearing the wisdom of Br. Lawrence,
St. Francis de Sales, St. Thérèse of Lisieux, Cardinal Joseph
Bernardin, Thomas Merton, and many others. From them
gradually I learned that looking for God in the most ordinary moments and making prayer the foundation of our
lives will eventually steer us toward the specific callings he
has planned for each of us.

By the early 2000s, precisely what that calling was for
me, however, remained outside the bounds of my awareness, even after several years of integrating monastic prin-
ciples into my life. Still, other measures of success mattered
more. Most importantly, my anxiety issues, which had
come so close to wrecking my life, were finally coming
under control. As my sense of balance and meaning grew,
the panic attacks and related symptoms faded, permitting
me to ease off medication after eighteen months. After a
couple years, only my longstanding fear of falling down in

public places remained, and by then even that old nemesis was losing its power.

One sure sign of improvement was my increasing preoccupation with finding a calling, which I'd not pondered for even a moment in the throes of anxiety. Reaching the age of thirty, I felt frustrated at times by my lack of a master plan. Many friends, it seemed, already had their careers as doctors, lawyers, and teachers mapped out, their families started, their mortgages arranged. Why couldn't I, too, figure out once and for all what I was here for?

And so I became acquainted with a final crucial stage of awareness: waiting. "What many of us detest, the monk spends a lifetime doing," writes Michael Downey in *Trappist*. "He waits for the God who comes sometimes in a moment of dazzling darkness but more often over the long haul of waiting things out."[2] Learning how to wait meant a couple things in particular for me. First, it freed me from the straitjacket of believing I couldn't move forward with my life at all until I had a grand plan worked out to the smallest details. Second, waiting didn't mean standing still. It meant moving ahead incrementally, making choices, seeing where they led, and making additional ones, while waiting for a fuller vision of the future to emerge. It meant proceeding, as Downey tells us, like the monk searching for God, "from hunch to hunch, hint after hint, by the whisper of a promise."[3]

So I forged ahead, unsure of exactly where I was going, but enjoying the journey far more than I had in the past. I left journalism to work for a Greensboro-based nonprofit specializing in leadership education. Dawn and I bought our first house, and, within a few months of moving into it, our first child was born.

About the time of my ten-year reunion at Duke, I started work on something I'd been pondering since the night
I'd learned of Dr. Fowlie's death—an essay that celebrated
his muscular example as a Catholic. It was a small way
of repaying a massive debt to my former professor—and
an opportunity to at least partially right the wrong I still
felt I'd committed by losing touch with him at the end of
his life. Working on that piece took me back through his
many books, prompted a search through several boxes of
his archived materials at Duke, and drew me closer to him
than I'd felt in years. *Commonweal* published the article in
the spring of 2006, launching a modest side pursuit for me
as an essayist.

By then my awareness had brought me to this realization: it's not only possible but preferable to have more than
one vocation in our lives, messy though it can be. Instead of
obsessing over a single life-changing call, I'd become comfortable with cultivating several as a family man, Catholic,
writer, professional, and overall pilgrim. It's not a perfect
life. The house gets overrun with toys and chaos. The kids
wake up in the middle of the night. The unending juggle
and competing demands of a two-career household strain
our patience. We worry about sick and aging family members, the illnesses and misfortunes visited upon friends and
acquaintances. Still, it's a way of being that feels deeply
right. Fr. Walter Ciszek observed that "the validity of a call
can be tested—whether it be the call of a vocation or of
some new departure within that vocation—by the movements of the soul that accompany it." More often than not,
the movements I sense are those of gratitude and joy and
peace—the kind that come from getting something you
really needed and knowing what it cost you down to the

last penny, the kind of wholesome lesson you might expect to learn in Mayberry.

PART TWO

A Path to Purpose

CHAPTER THREE

Desires: Digging for What You Really Want

FR. THOMAS BERRY WAS A ROMAN CATHOLIC PRIEST and world-renowned "ecotheologian." He devoted his ninety-four years to the passionate study and defense of the planet, contending that we cannot ultimately sustain ourselves as individuals or as a species without a thorough understanding and appreciation of the history of the universe. He founded and for more than two decades ran the Riverdale Center for Religious Research in the Bronx. He taught at Columbia, Fordham, and Seton Hall. He wrote award-winning books, including *The Dream of the Earth* and *The Great Work: Our Way into the Future*. His ideas and example powerfully influenced the environmental movement worldwide. Harvard's Archives for Environmental Science and Public Policy house his papers. By a strange coincidence, he found his calling about fifty yards from the front stoop of my house.

One day back in the 1920s, when Berry was just eleven years old, he went out to explore the open land and woods near his family's home in Greensboro, North Carolina. What he encountered at one particular instant on that sloping, grassy landscape changed his life:

> The field was covered with white lilies rising above the thick grass. A magic moment, this experience gave to my life something that seems to explain my thinking at a more profound level than almost any other experience I can remember. It was not only the lilies. It was the singing of the crickets and the woodlands in the distance and the clouds in a clear sky. . . . This early experience, it seems, has become normative for me throughout the entire range of my thinking. Whatever preserves and enhances this meadow in the natural cycles of its transformation is good; whatever opposes this meadow or negates it is not good. My life orientation is that simple.[1]

Nearly a century later, much of that meadow where Berry's vocation emerged is gone, cleared and paved long ago for a subdivision built for veterans returning from World War II. But it's not entirely lost either. His epiphany occurred very close to what is now the intersection of Brookside Drive and Colonial Avenue. It's a spot, in fact, that's cleanly visible from the small office in the house where I sometimes work from home. I usually drive or run or walk past it several times a day. What's left of Berry's meadow is a narrow strip of greenway alive with thick grass and speckles of flowers and a wall of trees and shrubs pressed right up against a creek that splits the land in two—just a shadow of its former splendor, but lovely nonetheless. When I pass by, it is usually work or shopping lists or worries about the kids on my mind, not Thomas Berry.

But occasionally I do think of him, of how what transpired in this ordinary spot on an ordinary day transformed a life and helped launch a global movement. I'm reminded of how the epic journey toward the people we're intended to become can start anywhere at any moment with desires that are impossible to predict and that define us as uniquely as our own fingerprints. When we have battled our way to the edge of the wilderness and have begun to feel awareness pulling us toward a purpose beyond mere survival, we do well to tend to our desires. Exploring them deeply and honestly is crucial for growing into our callings. Without a strong sense of what we really want, without some beginning sense of what God put us here to do, experienced as a real attraction, all the good intentions in the world won't do us a lot of good. In *The Jesuit Guide to (Almost) Everything*, Fr. James Martin writes of the foundational role of desires in our spiritual growth:

> Desire is a primary way that God leads people to discover who they are and what they are meant to do. On the most obvious level, a man and a woman feel physical, emotional and spiritual desire for each other, and in this way they discover their vocations to be married. A person feels an attraction to being a doctor or a lawyer or a teacher, and so discovers his or her vocation. Desires help us find our way. But first we have to know them.[2]

That can be an exciting challenge, as we explore likes and dislikes we'd perhaps only considered before at a surface level. Rather than trying to answer the overwhelming question of "What am I supposed to do with my life?" we can engage in a more manageable exercise sparked by a simple question: "What am I drawn toward?" and then see where that leads us. The key is to zero in on our authentic interests and to take them seriously, regardless of their apparent practicality or usefuleness. If we had a week in which we were totally free to do the things we enjoy, what would they be? At the same time, we should be aware that Americans, and for that matter residents of virtually any developed nation, live in a world that not only caters to our unchecked (and unexamined) desires but also tries incessantly and insidiously to tell us what our desires are, often creating desires where none previously existed. It's the fundamental role of advertising in all its forms—to make us crave those things we wouldn't otherwise want and to define success by our ability to attain them. Our recent national economic calamities were and are, at their core, the result of desire gone amuck—people splurged on houses and cars and vacations they couldn't really afford, banks loaned money against all common sense, supposed watchdogs looked the other way while an entire economic system propelled by borrowing and spending very nearly fell apart. It seems we let our wants go unexamined for far too long, and they got the best of us. It's true that desire can help us find our way. But it can also make us lose it.

The tension between healthy and unhealthy desire exists in all of us. Even Catholic monks experience it. "Personal and individual ambition seek to dominate the monk even in the midst of the monastic culture," observed Fr. Francis Kline, the late abbot of Mepkin Abbey. "The monastery frequently becomes a hell where the power of the fittest seems to hold sway. The juniors never seem to be listened to by the seniors. The seniors have no wish to change anything they have become accustomed to."[3] Even monks, who have given over their lives to the eradication of pride, can be run aground by their desires. In the end, though, what distinguishes them from many of us is their sense of perspective. "It is here in this land of yearning for more and yet more and even still more again, this geography of desire, that the Word of God evokes something in me, from me, for more than myself," Michael Downey writes in *Trappist*. "Throughout our lifetime this early, raw, sheer desire becomes more subtle. Through Word and Spirit it is purified and thereby inclines to what is worthy of our desiring."[4]

We all want what we want from a very young age. That impulse is not a terrible thing. It points us—however delicately and even haphazardly at times—in God's direction and gives us practice in wanting something with our whole hearts. The monk, while acknowledging the dangers of desire, maintains belief in its transformative power and takes the long view, accepting that we can't harness all of our desires immediately. Moving from purely selfish wants to authentic, life-giving ones is a journey that will last our entire lives. Prayer, reflection, and paying attention to the movements of our hearts are crucial for making progress, but along the way we're bound to do things of which we're not proud. This continual tension between selfish wants and authentic desires is a positive force; it keeps us from drifting too far toward aimless self-indulgence on the one extreme and excessive self-regard on the other.

Following our desires can unleash life-changing forces and also expose us to unwelcome distractions—and often we need time to make sense of the ensuing mess. Actor Martin Sheen's life offers one very public example. The son of Catholic immigrant parents, Ramon Gerardo Antonio Estevez landed a role in a local television commercial as a child in Dayton, Ohio. That was all it took to hook him on acting. Still, there was a problem: his left arm had been crushed by forceps during his birth, restricting its movement and also making it three inches shorter than his other arm. It wasn't exactly the look of a leading man. But Estevez had an even bigger problem than that: his father, a career employee with the National Cash Register Company, disapproved strongly of his son's would-be career.

Determined to follow his calling anyway, Estevez deliberately flunked an entrance exam to the University of Dayton. In 1959, he borrowed $500 from a parish priest who supported his acting aspirations and set off for New York City. There, surrounded by people who couldn't pronounce his name, he adopted the stage moniker of Martin Sheen, a blend of Robert Dale Martin, a casting director who gave him an early break, and Archbishop Fulton Sheen, a prominent Catholic televangelist.

From where Sheen sits now as an award-winning screen icon, devout Catholic, and fearless peace activist, his destiny seems as if it were preordained. Actually, all he had at the beginning was a strong sense of calling to the stage. Arriving in New York on a Greyhound bus at just eighteen years old, Sheen took a job as a stock boy at American Express to pay the bills while he searched for acting roles. His bosses didn't take kindly to all the time he missed while dashing around town for auditions. He was fired after about a year. Sheen did manage, however, to secure work as a stagehand and understudy with a radical theater company. They paid him a $5 a week, and, realizing he couldn't live on that, encouraged him to visit a friend of theirs who ran a soup kitchen on Chrystie Street. Its name: the Catholic Worker house. Their friend: legendary

Catholic journalist and social activist Dorothy Day, whom Sheen befriended.

"That was my invitation to social justice, and we've been connected ever since,"[5] says Sheen, who has been arrested literally dozens of times for civil disobedience at peace protests, has joined major immigration marches, has supported environmental rights groups, and has campaigned against abortion, capital punishment, and war. It wasn't until the late 1960s, nearly a full decade after he'd arrived in New York, that Sheen started regularly landing good television and movie roles, slowly steering him toward stardom and a lasting career in the craft he loves. It's worth remembering that just because Sheen nurtured his powerful and legitimate desire to act didn't mean his calling unfolded easily. He also battled destructive desires—struggles with alcohol, for example—that might easily have wrecked his life. As his career blossomed in the 1970s, he drank too much and lived too hard, leading to a heart attack on the set of the film *Apocalypse Now*. Even with that harsh wake-up call, however, it still took several more years for him to turn things around. Beyond all of its complexity and drama, however, Sheen's example points to an often underappreciated path toward knowing our desires—staying true to what enthralled us as children. I know from both growing up and from observing my own kids that it's never wise to put too much stock in the whims of children. Their interests and direction can change ten times in the course of an hour. Still, the things we are drawn to deeply in our youth can be very accurate markers of what we were made to do with our lives. We all know people who liked to draw and became architects, or liked taking things apart and became engineers, or ran a great

lemonade stand and went into sales. It's worth asking ourselves this question, no matter how old we are today: what
did I like most about being a kid? What were my dreams?
What happened to them?

This is not meant to be an exercise in nostalgia or an
excuse for pining about years and opportunities lost. It's
a simple technique that might just yield some worthwhile,
surprising insights—and get us thinking about what matters to us most. Sheen, for all his flaws through the first
half of his life, did not let go of a childhood dream that
he had every cause to abandon for reasons both practical
and familial. Yet, his tenacity and a real sense of purpose
led him deep into the acting career for which he yearned.
It also directly and quite serendipitously led him to the
Catholic Worker movement, giving greater shape and
voice to a passion for social justice he'd known since his
youth. In this way, he cultivated a twin calling as a Catholic
advocate for peace and justice that endures to this day. It
was a happy accident of sorts—or was it? I would argue
that following our authentic desires, while also trying hard
to cultivate goodness in our hearts, will open up expansive
and unexpected opportunities to love and serve. Either
way, it's a compelling case for taking our youthful desires
seriously throughout our lives.

Sheen was blessed, of course, to grasp his deepest
desires at a young age. That's not the case for many of us,
and trying to plumb childhood memories for clues to what
drives us, as helpful as that can be, will not yield results for
everyone. And that's okay. In his classic essay, "Managing

Oneself," Peter Drucker, the pioneer of modern management theory and practice, reminds us that

> a small number of people know very early where they belong. Mathematicians, musicians and cooks, for instance, are usually mathematicians, musicians and cooks by the time they are four or five years old. Physicians usually decide on their careers in their teens, if not earlier. But most people, especially highly gifted people, do not really know where they belong until they are well past their mid-twenties.[6]

Bob Johansen, author of the book *Leaders Make the Future*, once talked with Drucker about the keys to leadership and building organizational cultures in which talented people can grow. Drucker's advice is that we should test out a lot of different roles and work with many kinds of people during the first half of our lives (which Drucker defined as forty or fifty years), since we are not yet mature enough to know who we are. "In the second half of life," Johansen writes, "he said that people should only work on things they are passionate about and with people they admire. I found this very optimistic advice, since Drucker lived to be ninety-five and worked productively up to the end."[7]

Still, Drucker insisted on the importance of reflecting on our experiences in those wilderness years. It's not enough merely to have the experience; we also need to make sense of what we encounter during the first half of our lives. Even if we don't know where we belong, Drucker advises, we must be able to answer three critical questions: First, what are my strengths? Second, under what circumstances do I perform best? Finally, what are my values? Answering those questions thoroughly will help us decide where we belong in the world of work. I would submit they are also vital questions for getting at our real desires and, ultimately, our larger callings.

Tired of journalism in my twenties, for example, I briefly pondered earning an MBA and jumping into the corporate world. I was good at writing, but it didn't seem to be leading anywhere. Instead, I briefly envisioned myself as one of the movers and shakers I covered on the business beat. Plus, the money would be great! Fortunately, I asked myself a version of Drucker's three questions, and they helped uncover my real desires. Given my strengths, getting an MBA would have been a miserable experience. I've never enjoyed math and statistics. I'm also terrible at them. As far as ideal circumstances, the kind of executive jobs of which I dreamed involve lots of meetings. I hate meetings. They also require task forces and endless talking and haggling over budgets and resources. I like to get things done quietly, one-on-one or by myself. And when it comes to values, the truth is money has never been a key driver. I don't care much about status or having fancy, expensive toys. Objectively speaking, my greatest strength was writing, I liked working in small, closely-knit teams, and I wanted to join an organization that made a real difference. In the end, writing speeches for the CEO of a global nonprofit was a far better fit than coordinating earnings calls with reporters at a Fortune 500 company.

What happens, though, when our authentic desires don't reveal themselves easily or early? Here we can learn from esteemed-educator and bestselling-writer Parker Palmer. As a star student in high school and college, he created for himself (and for others who knew him) glowing expectations of great things to come—prestigious jobs, major leadership positions, a career defined by one success after another. It did not, however, work out that way.

Fresh out of college, Palmer planned to enter the ministry. He quickly discovered he disliked the studies and got lousy grades. So he moved on to the University of California at Berkeley to earn a PhD in sociology. It took him most of the 1960s to get the degree. When he finally did, he realized that the stultifying atmosphere of academia didn't suit him either. So he wound up in Washington, DC, as an assistant professor and full-time community organizer. This was the kind of work he thought he should be doing. It made a difference for the disenfranchised, took on the powers that be, and helped change some lives for the better. But even that didn't feel right. Burned out by the nonstop conflict the job entailed, he retreated to a small Quaker community in Pennsylvania for a yearlong sabbatical. By now he was in his mid thirties, lacking direction and still terribly unsure of his desires.

The one-year sabbatical turned into a ten-year stay as he became the Quaker community's dean of studies. It was an odd choice. Palmer, whose mentors had believed for years that he was on track for a college presidency, now found himself on the very fringe of academia in an obscure, experimental community. Friends and family thought he was nuts; Palmer couldn't blame them. What in the world was he doing with his life? Finally, there came what appeared to be his big break: a small, nearby college offered him its presidency. He'd already made up his mind to accept it but, in the Quaker tradition, convened a small group of friends for a "clearness committee," which is prohibited from giving advice but simply asks questions designed to help individuals make important decisions.

The questions went well until one person asked Palmer what he would like most about being president. "The simplicity of that question loosed me from my head and lowered me into my heart," Palmer writes. "I remember pondering for at least a full minute before I could respond." When he finally did, he succeeded only in listing the things he wouldn't like about the job—the politics and glad-handing and losing out on summer vacations:

> Once again the questioner called me back to the original question. But this time I felt compelled to give the only honest answer I possessed, an answer that came from the very bottom of the barrel, an answer that appalled even me as I spoke it. "Well," said I, in the smallest voice I possess, "I guess what I'd like most is getting my picture in the paper with the world *president* under it."[8]

It was a stunning revelation for Palmer to see the extent to which his desires—then and throughout his entire life up to that point—had to do with gratifying his ego instead of living authentically. No wonder he wasn't getting anywhere. But even then, struggles remained. Palmer endured two serious bouts of clinical depression in his forties. It was the natural consequence, he realized later, of living too much in his head, approaching his Christian faith too abstractly, and most of all feeding his all-consuming focus on "who I ought to be or what I ought to do, rather than by insight into my own reality, into what was true and possible and life-giving for me." Palmer discovered through his battles with depression that "one begins the slow walk back to health by choosing each day things that enliven one's selfhood and resisting things that do not."[9]

Palmer was well into middle age before he found a way out of his quagmire. That progress came about only because he was finally willing to pay attention to his own instincts and inner life, setting aside what the world deemed important and worthwhile. Understanding that he was energized by teaching but not built for the frustrations and vagaries of institutional life, he aligned himself as a consultant with associations that focused on improving university teaching. He stayed deeply connected to Quaker communities and began writing books about teaching and authenticity. Gradually he found his groove—ultimately winning recognition as one of the most influential senior leaders in higher education and carving out a niche as a popular author and speaker.

Palmer's example is both unsettling and uplifting in its implications. It reminds us of just how agonizingly long it can take for some of us to identify and to act on our authentic desires. At the same time, he shows us that it's never too late to begin or to recommit to the quest. Indeed, the older we get, the greater chance we might have of success. Palmer doesn't reference Peter Drucker, but he follows Drucker's recommended vocational path to the letter—spending the first half of his life experiencing a wide array of careers and interacting with extraordinarily different types of people, painful though it was. In the second half he zeroed in on his strengths as a teacher and writer, grasped that he works most effectively outside of organizational politics, and happily embraced values of integrity, balance, and faith that unlocked his potential.

If we're well into our thirties or forties or beyond and still vocationally at sea, cynicism abounds. If we really had a calling, we're probably asking, wouldn't we know it by now? There's also the matter of sheer exhaustion: I've been trying in many ways for many years to know my desires;

maybe it's time to give up. A key lesson we can draw from Palmer is to keep trying, to keep exposing ourselves to new ideas and new people, because there's always the potential at any moment, like Thomas Berry wandering in a sunny field, that something will suddenly click. That might not mean walking away from a career with no backup plan or taking a long, exotic vacation. How many of us have the money for that? Still, we might do something as simple as sign up for a single college course on a topic that piques our interest. We could attempt an athletic feat that has always seemed out of reach, like running a 5K race.

Meanwhile, we'll need to complement our accumulation of experience with regular reflection on it. Many of us have little or no patience for pausing long enough to take stock. Others, like me, are prone to excessive introspection. Either way, we need to take the onus off ourselves. Palmer's insights, after all, didn't just come of his own accord. They were largely the result of feedback he received from those who cared for him—"clearness committees," mentors, and family members. More than receiving advice we'll probably ignore, we need people around us who are good at asking questions and even better at listening to our answers and asking more questions. Nobody can find someone else's truth for them, but wise people can be great guides and motivators who lead us to the brink of lasting realizations.

Who are the wise people in your life? If you know, reach out to them. Let them challenge you with questions and give real thought to the answers. There are few things more potentially painful than dealing with our messy inner lives. It's much easier, frankly, to take a nap or drink a beer or watch a football game until the most recent wave of incompleteness passes. But if that inner work isn't done, we will never fully know our desires. We will never know what we're capable of doing or what it means to feel the call to do it.

.∽∽⌒⌒∽.

Heeding our childhood instincts as Martin Sheen did or edging our way toward awareness over time in the fashion of Parker Palmer are two tested ways of tuning into our desires. There is plenty to recommend both. Their potential downside, however, is that they require spending a lot of time thinking about ourselves. An intense focus on our inner lives is absolutely necessary at times, but it also comes with the risk of self-absorption. We can get so fixated on our inner quest, even when our intentions are entirely good, that the search for authentic desires becomes counterproductive. Sometimes we need the flexibility to allow external circumstances or the needs of others to jolt us out of circular reverie—and lead us to a better understanding of our desires at the same time.

By the time of her death in 1980, Dorothy Day, whose lasting influence on Sheen we have already noted, was already regarded as a modern-day saint—one of the most influential, intriguing, and inspiring Catholics of her time. Her Catholic Worker movement, conceived and directed by lay people, showed Church officials and the world at large what it looks like to live out the Gospel uncompromisingly—forsaking worldly ambitions, sheltering and feeding the sick and poor, standing up against even the most popular wars, and advocating for a new social order through journalism, prayer, and tight-knit community.

Day's ending was a long way from the bohemian life-style of her twenties. Day had spent those years enmeshed with communists, radicals, and liberal writers, most of whom mocked religion, in Karl Marx's phrase, as the opiate of the masses. They saw revolution, rather than prayer, as the likeliest path to change as they wrote, protested, and drank their way through the Prohibition Era. In later years, Day deeply regretted those years lost to what she considered waywardness and amorality. How did she start the journey from there to her sanctified spot in the Catholic imagination? In a word, motherhood.

Day had always felt her desires deeply, whatever they were. As she neared age thirty, she had found her niche as a secular radical of sorts, a journalist committed to serving the masses and upending the corrupt social order that oppressed them. She and her common-law husband, Forster Batterham, moved from New York City out to Staten Island, where they cultivated a simple life of deep thought and conversation, a life of protest against what they viewed as a greedy, war-mongering, heartlessly capitalistic world. Then Day became pregnant. It was, as she writes in her autobiography, *The Long Loneliness*, a time of "blissful joy"—in large part because she'd feared being unable to have a child and also because she felt incomplete without one. Around the same time, mysteriously and despite her deep-seated doubts about religion, she began praying regularly. She was horrified at first, not the least because she viewed formal religion and Catholicism in particular as among the pillars of the unjust status quo. She started to realize, however, that she wasn't conversing with God out of desperation or greed; she was actually praying purely out of thanks.

When her daughter Tamar Teresa was born in 1926, it didn't take Day long to decide to have her baptized Catholic. In doing so, Day, who had been alternately strongly attracted and repelled by religion up to that point, came down decisively in its favor. Unlike many of her radical friends, she had a strong spiritual dimension—and, despite the fact that the struggling masses were not held in much esteem by many clergy and middle-class Catholics, she believed that the Catholic Church really was the Church of her beloved poor. "No human creature could receive or contain so vast a flood of love and joy as I often felt after the birth of my child," she writes. "With this came the need to worship, to adore." Though she was thoroughly unschooled in Catholicism, joining it was an option that appealed powerfully to her. "I loved the Church for Christ made visible," she writes.[10]

The problem was that she also loved Batterham intensely—and knew her conversion to Catholicism would drive away the love of her life and father of her child. As an anarchist and atheist, Batterham thought religion a farce that wasted lives and devalued the beauty and truths of the natural world. It was a bitter irony for Day "who always felt that it was life with him that brought me natural happiness, that brought me to God." She continued to prepare surreptitiously for her own entrance into the Church and tried desperately to change his mind about the compatibility of her love for him and for God, painfully stalling the inevitable end. The agony stretched on into the summer of 1927, with Batterham withdrawing more and more and Day on the verge of a nervous breakdown:

> By winter the tension had become so great that an explosion occurred and we separated again. When

> he returned, as he always had, I would not let him
> in the house; my heart was breaking with my own
> determination to make an end, once and for all, to
> the torture we were undergoing.[11]

The next morning she was baptized Catholic and made her first confession. The day after that, she received Communion for the first time. The year ahead was a hard one, marked by uncertainty, illness, and continued mourning of her split with Batterham. But she had finally zeroed in on her most fundamental desires: to grow as a Catholic, to raise her daughter, and to pursue social justice through writing and service. What that would look like in practice would in fact remain somewhat murky for several years, until she met itinerant philosopher Peter Maurin. In 1933 they founded the *Catholic Worker* newspaper to shine a light on the links between the Church teachings and social justice; their controversial social movement followed thereafter. Day had tracked her desires all the way into the start of a world-changing vocation.

Day's life is a testament to having the flexibility to follow our evolving desires. She embraced a bohemian lifestyle wholeheartedly until she began to see it didn't work for her anymore. She committed herself unreservedly to Forster Batterham until she saw that romantic love alone was not enough to sustain her. Even after she entered the Church, subtle shifts occurred.

At first, for example, it was a battle just to establish baseline knowledge of her new faith. For a while after that, it was enough to pray and go to Mass and write about social justice for Catholic magazines. Later, she felt the powerful urge to start her own newspaper and make it the focal point of a radically Christ-centered community.

At no point, really, did she strike poses or deceive herself or act hypocritically. Her desires changed with the seasons of her life, and the growing wisdom that accompanied those shifts surely helped mold her into the force she's remembered as now. By letting her desires lead her, rather than trying to cram them into neatly organized boxes, Day ensured that she never lived in a bubble of introspection or excessive self-certainty. She allowed the outside world to interrupt, to steer her in startling and not always entirely pleasant directions. In so doing, she cultivated a capacity for surprise and unexpected growth that was essential to her calling.

How do we develop greater flexibility in service of our vocational desires? Though I never did earn an MBA, I'm still partial to what they refer to in the business world as "real-options analysis." As academics Lenos Trigeorgis, Rainer Brosch, and Han Smit explained it in the *Wall Street Journal*, "instead of making rock-hard plans and irreversible long-term commitments, the idea is to create flexibility by breaking decisions down into stages."[12]

For example, if a company wants to build a new factory, it might, in the name of efficiencies and scale, decide to build the biggest one it can afford. Or, because it's very difficult to assess the future beyond a year or two, it could put up a smaller factory that is also designed for expansion. In the latter scenario, if business deteriorates, executives have a smaller plant that could be closed without a huge financial hit. If business picks up, the option always exists to make the factory bigger.

Similarly, Day never locked herself into one static version of her desires that would fail her when the circumstances of her life changed, as they inevitably would. She always felt the pain of the marginalized and was driven to make the world a better place for them. But she didn't say, "The single best way for me to do this is as an anarchist bohemian," or, "I'll focus solely on documenting social injustice in Catholic magazines." Rather, she made choices that opened up more choices. It wasn't clear for several years after her conversion how her passions for writing, activism, and Catholicism might blend. It was an uncertain time, surely frustrating for her, that involved juggling motherhood with cross-country moves and an array of jobs. Still, she honored each of these desires by moving more deeply into each of them. Ultimately, they integrated perfectly into the Catholic Worker movement, whose sum impact would have been much less without all three parts.

Sheen, Palmer, and Day represent three distinct ways of cultivating our truest desires. Many of us, however, will find ourselves enlisting all three approaches at different stages in our lives. By the time I was ten years old, I understood the real pleasure that writing a good sentence or reading a good book brought. Then, as now, there was little else that compared, and it was a blessing to know at a young age what inspired me. But just as Parker Palmer knew early on that he loved teaching but could never find quite the right way to pursue it, I struggled for a long time to figure out what role writing should play in my life.

At first I thought I might utilize it as a lawyer; a bit later it seemed the right skill for a career in academia. Finally, out of college and needing a job, I went into newspaper journalism. What could be more writing-intensive than that? But the money and hours were exceptionally bad, and, even worse, the relentless grind of cranking out one story after another for years on end nearly killed my love of writing altogether. It took until well into my thirties—and a lot of painful second-guessing—to finally recognize I could make a living and still keep my interest in the craft fresh by continually alternating among many different kinds of writing—speeches and personal essays and newspaper columns and business pieces. Even organizational memos offered a nice change of pace.

In somewhat similar fashion to Day, I came to this more advanced realization of my desires largely because of a major outside event that snapped me out of self-absorption and brooding—the arrival of children. Suddenly there were more bills and more money needed to pay them. Being an in-house writer, which we'd all scorned as journalists, didn't seem so beneath me anymore. Free time, which I'd squandered shamelessly throughout my twenties, barely existed now. If I was serious about my own writing projects, which I'd pondered for years with no action, they needed to be squeezed into whatever twenty-minute increments were available. So that's what I did and continue to do now. The quest for our authentic desires is a messy endeavor—astonishingly haphazard and sideways, a map of territory gained and lost and won back again. When we commit ourselves to it wholeheartedly, however, we lay the groundwork on which enduring callings are built.

CHAPTER FOUR

Focus: Channeling Your Passions

LIKE MOST PEOPLE, I'VE HAD A FEW INTIMIDATING teachers over the years. First came Mr. Smith, who taught fourth grade but cast a shadow all the way down the long hall to the kindergarten classrooms. Tall, mustached, and known for his hair-trigger temper, he had students in the lower grades at Leaders Heights Elementary School shaking in their shoes. If it was his turn to monitor the gym while we waited for the buses at the end of the day, you kept your mouth shut. Completely. "Anyone want a size fourteen shoe stuffed down their throat?" he snarled at us one afternoon, back in the days when public-school teachers could say such things, many parents encouraged it, and the possibility of it actually happening seemed reasonably high.

In high school, it was Mr. Cleary, the resident football coach/philosophy teacher whose massive upper body looked ready to pop the tie straight off his shirt if he so much as sneezed. "All right," he'd say, biceps rippling, buff shoulders rolling beneath his suit vest, while stroking his menacing goatee, "does anyone recall the meaning of Occam's razor?" Jaded though we were as seventeen-year-old seniors, our instant response was to rip through our notebooks for the answer. If he called on one of us and we responded incorrectly, it seemed entirely possible that he could simply lift his hand like Darth Vader and strangle us from halfway across the room.

In college, no one compared to Reynolds Price, internationally acclaimed novelist and memoirist, Rhodes Scholar, and iconic member of Duke University's English department. Bound to a wheelchair by a spinal tumor that had nearly killed him in the 1980s, Price couldn't stand up to make a point. He didn't need to. I'd pick up one of his many books from time to time, and there he'd be on the jacket grinning and affable beneath a wave of whitish hair, as if to say, "Why don't you drop in during office hours and we'll share a laugh!" It was an image totally incongruous with the Price I knew as an undergrad.

I'll never forget joining a couple of buddies during my sophomore year for the annual Founders' Day celebration in Duke Chapel. It was a ceremony devoted to extolling the university's traditions and achievements. Just the year before, novelist William Styron had waxed eloquent about his glorious undergraduate years at Duke. We filed into our seats on that afternoon in December 1992 expecting the same from Price, the event's keynote speaker. He'd barely cleared his throat, however, before declaring, "I defy any of you to ride the bus from East Campus to West and hear a remark of any greater intellectual consequence than, 'I can't believe how drunk I was last night.'" The rout was on, as Price blasted the university and all of its members for failing to create the oasis of learning envisioned by its founders. My friends and I sat there slack-jawed, like everyone around us. Price's talk sparked a university-wide discussion that led to numerous reforms.

Even as I cowered in their midst, however, all three of these men gradually became sources of lasting inspiration and wisdom. Indeed, they are on the short list of the very best teachers I was ever privileged to have. One of their biggest lessons: order, effort, and follow-through matter immensely if we are to fulfill our potential. In the end, these teachers succeeded in part because they felt called to teaching, and we could sense that. They had zeroed in on this desire and dedicated themselves wholly to it.

But plenty of people have an authentic urge to teach. Only a small percentage of them are truly memorable. What makes the difference? In that field as in most others, I would say it's the ability to transform pure, unfiltered passion—our most fundamental desires, in other words— into concrete, sustained actions that shape those desires and direct their growth. Simply put, we need focus. A new teacher can have a burning wish to change lives in the classroom. A young married couple can say in all sincerity their love will always last. An executive can vow to reform the negative, spiteful culture of her business. But unless there's a day-to-day plan and larger structure for how that's going to happen, it probably won't. Like tomato plants that burst out of the ground in early summer and soon collapse under their own weight if not carefully staked, our desires can falter and die without deliberate cultivation.

My best teachers never let that happen. They all exhibited exceptional intensity and concentration and were highly demanding of themselves. They knew that was the key to great performance. They could be hard on us because they wanted our best as well. More specifically, they understood that meaning does not simply emerge out of chaos; it requires structure.

Mr. Smith, for instance, was the only teacher in the school who saw that the natural energy of fourth graders needed channeling—and did something about it. Many mornings after we'd settled at our desks and listened to the opening announcements, he'd tell us to stand up and go outside. There, in the wet morning grass, we'd run a few joyful laps around the school while he urged us on. We'd return to the classroom, sneakers squeaking, a bit sweaty and out of breath, but ready to sit and learn. Nobody else did that, which made him not only the scariest but also the coolest guy in the school. Focus, too, meant effort, actually making time for the things we say are important.

In high school, Mr. Cleary insisted we find room for contemplation in our busy lives. And when even a few students showed interest, despite his duties as department chairman and father of a young family, he started showing up early at school to run a philosophy club. Focus also meant follow-through, keeping in touch with students past and present. I'd been gone from Duke for more than a decade when I e-mailed Price about an essay I'd published on Wallace Fowlie, my college mentor. Though he knew me vaguely at best, Price wrote back within hours thanking me for the message and requesting a copy of the piece. That's an e-mail I'll never delete.

Initially, I planned to title this chapter "discipline." It's a trait embodied by Smith, Cleary, Price, and many other people I admire, those with the persistence to run five miles a day or wake up early to meditate or unfailingly choose the salad bar over the burger station—the very kind of nose-to-the-grindstone mindset that seems necessary to channel our scattered desires into measurable, positive movement toward our callings. The fact is, however, I wasted a lot of time from about second grade until well into adulthood drawing up detailed daily schedules for spurring self-improvement. I'd plunge into this work wholeheartedly, getting up early to run laps around my parents' big backyard, forsaking Fruit Loops for yogurt at snack time, and doing my homework in the precise time allotted for it.

But by day three, I'd pretty much abandoned the whole project, finding myself pulled back far too easily into the old, comfortably unambitious routine. When I grew up, the same cycle repeated itself, only now at greater cost in the form of unused gym memberships and overlooked fruit going bad in the back of the refrigerator. None of that would come as a surprise to Tony Schwartz, a bestselling author who specializes in the study of human performance. "Will and discipline are wildly overrated," Schwartz writes in *The Way We're Working Isn't Working*. "That's why we struggle so hard to make changes that last."[1] As Schwartz explains, an astounding 95 percent of our behaviors result out of sheer habit.

How can this be, particularly among Americans who pride themselves on taking charge of their lives? It turns out that our heroic efforts at self-discipline typically fail because they demand heavy involvement from our brain's prefrontal cortex, where our capacity for deliberate self-regulation resides. The problem is that the prefrontal cortex's overall capacity is pretty limited. So the more we have to think about specific changes, the more likely our valiant

attempts at the self-control needed to enact them will fall
short. This explains why the vast majority of us fail to stick
with diets over the long term, don't make healthy changes
to our lifestyles even after suffering heart attacks, and
almost never see progress despite making the same New
Year's resolutions ten separate times.

Our reserves of willpower are pathetically low, and it's
not even our fault. It's just how our brains are wired. As
Schwartz notes, "We're often better served by replacing
our negative habits, formed in the more primitive parts of
our brain, with positive rituals—highly specific behaviors
that become automatic over time."[2] Perhaps a critical element we need then in pursuit of our callings is not so much
self-discipline, in the old iron-fisted, teeth-gritting sense of
the word, as an ability to focus steadily on our top priorities
until they become second nature. I won't attempt to sum-
marize here all of Schwartz's work. But in exploring how
to develop positive rituals, he offers some tips that seem of
considerable value in the quest to focus our desires.

The first key is to start small and build gradually from
there. Since we're not endowed with a lot of self-control,
it's simply not possible to make a lot of changes all at once.
We should pick one or two areas, develop very precise
steps for how we're going to cultivate them, and then stick
with it until these behaviors become habits. "Embedding a
ritual can take anywhere from a couple of weeks to several
months," Schwartz writes. "Even then, it's possible to build
several rituals over the course of a year, one at a time." In
building these rituals, however, we can expect to face resistance from ourselves along the way; never underestimate
the allure of the status quo. In Schwartz's words, "Because
we mostly fail to recognize the fears that are inevitably

associated with change, we often end up unconsciously sabotaging our own efforts to change."[3]

Finally, even as we attempt to make positive behaviors automatic, we have to pause and reflect now and then on whether they are still serving their original purpose. Have our lives developed in such a way that those behaviors are still valuable, or is it time to create new ones that better align with our present situation? We're called to master a "delicate dance between awareness and automaticity."

Trappist monks know the complex steps of this dance as well as anyone. For them, focus is absolutely essential to spiritual maturation, which balances an ever-present mindfulness with a highly trained body and brain that perform instinctively. All it takes to see that is a glance at their schedule. Their days begin with community prayers at 3:00 a.m. and end with bedtime at 8:00 p.m., with a busy, prescribed pattern of prayer, work, and study in between— and this is repeated day after day, year after year. It is a formula grounded in the Rule of St. Benedict, a sixth-century monk who shaped Western monasticism. According to St. Benedict's ancient directives, focus in a monastery starts with rationing food and sleep so as to ensure monks are healthy. However, neither food nor sleep is indulged in to an exent that most of us would consider comfortable. "Universal religious tradition has always taught that if you want to monitor the spiritual journey, you must begin with the body and the control of its appetites, especially the necessities," writes Fr. Francis Kline. "In the Christian tradition, there is no awakening of the spiritual realities without a concomitant response in the body. We are both exterior body and interior person. Our personhood cannot be divided."[4]

Most of us, with job and family responsibilities, cannot imitate the demanding daily routine of monks and probably would not choose to do so even if we could. Still, we can learn a great deal about focus from their example. Perhaps most significantly, we can accept that a certain amount of tension in our lives, a steady tug between a yearning to rest and a compulsion to push ourselves, is both productive and necessary. We can also recognize the importance of structure in our lives, that most of us thrive within the framework of routines. Like the lines on a tennis court, our routines force us to play within certain bounds. But we still have plenty of freedom to decide just how creatively we will operate in that space. And, of course, there's the indisputable proof that an exceptionally focused life pays off. How many other enterprises can you name that, like the Trappist order, have successfully adapted to all of the changes wrought by the passage of a thousand years?

Cardinal Joseph Bernardin did not fully grasp the power of focus until middle age. But when he did, it changed the trajectory of his life. Bernardin became well-known in the 1990s when, as the archbishop of Chicago, he endured a series of personal tragedies. First, he was accused of sexual abuse and had to endure months of suspicion before his accuser retracted the claims. Not long after that, he learned he had pancreatic cancer. Against considerable odds, surgery gave him a clean bill of health, and Bernardin was soon back to his busy schedule, which now included a special focus on ministering to individuals and families struggling with cancer. Then, just when Bernardin was beginning to embrace this new ministry, news came in August 1996 that the cancer had spread to his liver. Declining to pursue further treatment for an illness that now looked almost certainly fatal, Bernardin focused his final days on serving and setting a remarkable example for the sick and dying. That work included writing *The Gift of Peace,* a bestseller that he completed just two weeks before his death in November 1996.

Early in the book, Bernardin revealed something that surely surprised many admirers of his seemingly sterling spirituality: his prayer life had faltered midway through his distinguished pastoral career. It wasn't because his faith had flagged in any way; it was simply that his hectic schedule as a rising, highly regarded churchman had become so full he wasn't making time for his interior life. Or, in Bernardin's words, "I fell into the trap of thinking my good works were more important than prayer."[5]

One night, during dinner with several young priests, he confessed to this problem. "In very direct—even blunt terms—they helped me realize that as a priest and a bishop I was urging a spirituality on others that I was not fully practicing myself. That was a turning point in my life," he writes.[6] His solution—spend the first hour of each day in prayer, a ritual he started in the mid-1970s and never relinquished. That initial commitment was, as Robert Ellsberg describes it, "the beginning of a quiet process of conversion, marked by prayer and reflection on the cross that transformed a successful churchman into a man of God and prepared him for the trials that were to come."[7]

Bernardin succeeded in reclaiming his prayer life for a couple key reasons. First, he kept his approach simple and realistic. He did not, for example, design an elaborate plan that called for saying rosaries in the morning, engaging in contemplative prayer at lunch, doing spiritual reading in the middle of the afternoon, and conducting an examination of conscience before bedtime. Second, he was very specific about what he was going to do. Rather than pledging vaguely to make room for more prayer, he vowed to do it at the start of every day for an hour. And though he probably decided this without consulting modern neuroscience, he nevertheless adopted the kind of precision and consistency our brains need to build lasting rituals. That, in turn, made it possible to shift his abstract desire for a richer spiritual life into concrete practice. As Schwartz reminds us, "Often, when we make a commitment to a new behavior such as exercising, we fail to recognize that unless we set aside a specific time to do it, it's unlikely we will."[8] It was a trap Bernardin instinctively avoided.

Apart from his well-constructed ritual, Bernardin also armed himself with additional incentive for following through. He made a promise to a group of people whom he respected and that he knew would hold him accountable for results. The impact of this move should not be underestimated. Christians, particularly Catholics, ground their worship in communal rituals.

The Catholic Mass, for example, is ritualized such that you can go to virtually any church in the world on any given Sunday and still experience many key elements in common. A key part of that ritual involves standing with others as we profess our faith, confess our sins, and vow to do better. Would it be equally as powerful to voice the same commitment alone in an empty church? Even a hardcore introvert like me has to acknowledge that, no, it would not. And yet, when we head from church back into our daily routines, the matter of our private prayer lives can quickly become just that—totally private and sealed off from the rest of the world. In building our personal rituals, we should look to frame that work in a larger context—and draw inspiration from the challenges and support provided by other people.

In our own lives, there's no shortage of opportunities to try building a good ritual. It could be something directly related to desires we are trying to bring into greater focus, or something more general but important—diet, exercise, volunteer work, time with our families. I, for instance, had been writing essays for Catholic magazines for several years but was only engaging in substantive prayer intermittently—a few weeks of centering prayer here, some sporadic days of lectio divina there. Like Bernardin, I was busy.

In my defense, having two young children awake at all hours of the day and night made it hard, if I wanted to stay married, to tell my wife, "Come hell or high water, I'm devoting the first hour of every day to prayer!" Excuses aside, however, it gradually became apparent that I would not continue to generate good ideas or deliver useful insights in my writing if I didn't ground that work in a richer practice of prayer. About that time, I read Fr. James Martin's *Jesuit Guide to (Almost) Everything*. He explained the Jesuit examen—a nighttime prayer that involves reviewing our day in detail, noting the moments that made us grateful and the ones where we faltered, asking for forgiveness where necessary, and pledging to make progress the next day.

This was a realistic regimen that I enjoyed doing. It took fifteen minutes or fewer each day as well, not quite the investment Bernardin had made but still a significant change—one that has given my prayer life much greater consistency and focus over the past year. There is, of course, still a lot of room for improvement, so in the coming year (and probably the rest of my life!) prayer will remain the key area in which I seek small, gradual improvements.

Building positive rituals can slowly and surely help harness the power of our desires and move us deeper into our callings. Still, no matter the level of our commitment, we should expect to encounter obstacles to maintaining these rituals. Those obstacles might come from within ourselves—through the sort of subconscious self-sabotage observed by Schwartz, in which we deny ourselves what we've long sought just as we're on the verge of obtaining it. Or trouble could come entirely unexpectedly from the outside. No one knew this better than Agnes Gonxha Bojaxhiu. She left home at age eighteen to join the Sisters of Our Lady of Loreto and was assigned to teach at the convent's school in Calcutta. Following her desire to honor God brought her real meaning and satisfaction, and the rituals of faith she found in her order kept her focused. She worked hard and seemed quite content with the nearly twenty years she'd spent teaching middle-class students. Then came September 10, 1946. Riding a train from Calcutta to Darjeeling for a retreat, Sr. Agnes, not previously given to mystical encounters, felt an overwhelming, direct call from Jesus. He wanted her to serve India's sick and dying. "Wouldst thou not help?" Jesus asked her in a vision. "Wilt thou refuse me?" She was thirty-six years old.

Her newfound calling was fueled by a tremendously powerful and ambitious desire—to become a direct channel of Christ's love on a broken planet. Sr. Agnes's goals did not involve changing the entire world, but they were daring in their own specificity: to offer compassion and a measure of dignity to the homeless and naked and starving in the gutters of Calcutta—a city torn by riots—by living with them in poverty. They were so daring, in fact, that church officials didn't know what to make of her. Indeed, their skepticism became her first obstacle to this calling. She overcame it with a relentless letter-writing campaign to her local archbishop for approval to start her work.

It took nearly a year and a half of persuasion, but, after consulting with the Vatican, Sr. Agnes was finally allowed to begin. Her startling embodiment of charity quickly attracted followers. Together, they established the Missionaries of Charity, and Sr. Agnes became known as Mother Teresa. Over decades, her work caught the world's eye, and her selflessness made her a living saint, the recipient of the Nobel Peace Prize, and heroine of countless books and documentary films. When I was in high school in the late 1980s and talk turned to the most inspirational leaders we could name, it always came down to the "Big Three": Gandhi, Martin Luther King Jr., and Mother Teresa.

But as her letters to several spiritual directors later showed, the initial bliss afforded by her new vocation quickly yielded to another, far more daunting challenge—decades of spiritual darkness. The depths to which she plunged were almost entirely unknown until a series of tormented letters surfaced after her death in 1997. From the late 1940s—starting almost precisely when she began her work in the streets of Calcutta—until the end of her life, Mother Teresa suffered from a nearly crippling sense of separation from God. Doubt, isolation, and inner pain plagued her, even as her reputation and influence expanded enormously. "Please pray specially for me that I may not spoil His work and that Our Lord show Himself—for there is such terrible darkness within me, as if everything was dead," she admitted in one such letter.[9]

As she radiated faith, peace, and humility to the wider world, Mother Teresa waited for her troubles to lift. After a decade of anguish, the darkness suddenly vanished for five weeks. Then it returned, never to abate. Incredibly, it seems this unending trial, rather than diminishing her faith in God, became central to the fulfillment of Mother Teresa's calling. As scholar Carol Zaleski has written, "It would be her Gethsemane, she came to believe, and her participation in the thirst Jesus suffered on the Cross. And it gave her access to the deepest poverty of the modern world: the poverty of meaninglessness and loneliness."[10] How did Mother Teresa remain faithful to her desire to serve God in a profoundly counter-cultural fashion and maintain her focus through these years of spiritual torment? Like Bernardin, she started by opening up about her problems to a trusted friend, who offered some good advice in return. The Reverend Joseph Neuner, a respected theologian, became her confidant more than a decade into her spiritual dryness. Unlike her prior confessors, some of whom never comprehended the extent of her tribulations, Neuner "seems to have told her three things she needed to hear" about her darkness, according to journalist David Van Biema.[11]

First, this trial wasn't her fault and there wasn't much she could do about it. Second, just because she could not feel Jesus' presence as she had before, it did not mean he'd abandoned her. Third, contending with this painful void was a core part of her calling. "This counsel clearly granted Teresa a tremendous sense of release," Van Biema writes. "For all that she had expected and even craved to share in Christ's Passion, she had not anticipated that she might recapitulate the particular moment on the Cross when he asks, "My God, My God, why have you forsaken me?" The idea that rather than a nihilistic vacuum, his felt absence might be the ordeal she had prayed for, that her perseverance in its face might echo his faith unto death on the Cross . . . made sense of her pain."[12]

And that seemed to settle it for her. Though she never again felt the powerful connection to Jesus that she'd experienced in the early days of her ministry, she continued to go about her routine, day after day, for decades. By putting the challenges to her rituals of deep prayer and radical service in context, Mother Teresa preserved the rituals themselves from harm and recommitted herself to investing in them continually.

In similar circumstances, many of us would likely conclude the ritual itself is broken and abandon it in frustration. We might, after that annual lecture from our family doctor, for example, decide it really is time to take off some weight. So we start exercising and eating much more deliberately. We make daily appointments at the gym and plan out our meals carefully each day. We get some friends to join us and keep us motivated. These rituals pay off—over the first six months, we lose thirty pounds. We feel great, our friends notice we have more energy, our colleagues at work commend us for making better decisions. Month seven of our new regimen, however, isn't quite as rewarding. We only lose a pound. In month eight, we gain a couple. Now we're getting frustrated. We're doing the same things we've been doing all along—why the heck aren't they working as well?

Gradually, over weeks, we begin deconstructing our rituals. We eat pizza twice a week instead of just once. We make it to the gym two times instead of four. Suddenly, we're in the full throes of the resistance about which Schwartz has warned us. We're also at a crucial decision point. We can give up on the entire project. That's what most people do—and it's what keeps the diet industry in business. Or we can take a broader view. In Mother Teresa's case that meant realizing the waning personal connection she felt with Jesus wasn't the only gauge of her progress. She was also growing in humility and spiritual wisdom. She was building a religious order that modeled Christ's example, made a real difference in Calcutta, and inspired humanitarian work around the world. Likewise, we might say the number on the scale isn't the only measure of our progress either. As a result of embracing a ritual of healthier living, we're fitter than we had been, we feel better, and we're more productive—all good reasons to keep doing what we're doing even during the days or larger stretches when it's difficult.

Over the long run, however, there's more to increasing our focus than simply building rituals and fighting through the inevitable resistance to them. We also need to stay fresh and inspired—and that is a real challenge because it often calls for us to take a formula that's working and disrupt it, with the risk of introducing more flaws than enhancements. Still, it's a gamble we need to take periodically if we want to stay sharp and motivated. Fitness coaches know this truth well, and it's why they encourage their clients to cross-train. Instead of doing four runs of three miles every week, for example, they might recommend we keep things interesting by substituting some bike riding or swimming or weightlifting. One reason, of course, is that more variety means we won't get bored as easily and give up our exercise routine altogether. A second reason is that we're less likely to hurt ourselves by training one part of our body too hard and letting the rest of it go untended.

In our own lives, making adjustments to rituals before we grow restless could mean surrendering a positive but aging approach for an entirely new one. A friend of mine did this in rather dramatic fashion when he walked away from a promising law career to become a middle school teacher. My mom acted on a smaller scale when she left the local church she had been closely connected to for twenty years and joined another one across town because she found it more spiritually invigorating.

Staying fresh can also involve altering, rather than completely leaving behind, a ritual that has proven successful. Renowned executive-coach Marshall Goldsmith discovered the value of keeping rituals flexible as he attempted to become a better father. Stung by his daughter's observation that he never spent real time with her even when they were in the house together, Goldsmith started tracking the numbers of days each year in which he spent at least four hours with his family, free of television, cell phones, and other distractions. The first year he reached ninety-two days. By the fourth year, he was up to one hundred thirty-five. Wanting to improve even more, he suggested one hundred fifty days as his new goal. His kids, now well supplied in time with Daddy, requested that he instead scale it back to fifty. "I wasn't discouraged by their response," he says. "I was so focused on the numbers, on improving my at-home performance each year, that I forgot that my kids had changed, too. An objective that made sense when they were nine years old didn't make sense when they evolved into teenagers."[13] Before we congratulate ourselves too much on a well-entrenched ritual, we're wise to ask ourselves if we're not similarly overlooking circumstances that have changed.

Of course, for the most diehard creatures of habit among us, there's an alternative to retiring or updating our favorite rituals. We can maintain them while adding some new ones to the mix. My role model here is Bono, front man of the legendary Irish rock band, U2. *The Joshua Tree*, the band's Grammy-winning album from the 1980s, was an enormous achievement. Quiet, serious, and musically spare, it tunneled inside the minds of drug addicts, convicted killers, tortured lovers, and grieving parents. The record cemented U2's reputation as a smart band with an unusually strong social conscience.

Imagine the surprise, then, when the band released *Achtung Baby* in the fall of 1991. Slickly produced, loud, and startlingly unpolitical, its new sound caught fans off guard, as did Bono's new look. No longer a tortured artist howling about the hypocrisy of US-funded military operations in Central America, he'd suddenly morphed into a larger-than-life entertainer with a penchant for wearing oversized sunglasses and adopting an on-stage persona known as "the Fly." I loved the new record from the first listen in my freshman dorm at Duke, and I still do. Some of my friends instantly hated it—and still do. They thought U2 had sold out for commercial success, dumbing down lyrics and abandoning a decade of social activism. I thought the band had gone in a different direction because it didn't have a choice. *The Joshua Tree* was so good that there was little chance U2 could ever make a better album of that type. Its ritual of making serious music needed some reinvention.

Even as making music remained the band's primary occupation, Bono started branching out with additional rituals. In the late 1990s, he decided to do something about the plight of millions of Africans afflicted with drought, hunger, and disease. Steeping himself in the best ways to improve the continent's future, he leveraged his celebrity to become an international advocate for debt relief. This mission took him to Capitol Hill and government chambers around the world, where he successfully lobbied politicians to cancel loan payments owed by the poorest African nations so they could instead invest the money in health, education, and economic development.

For more than a decade, Bono has remained a leading spokesman for this cause, in which he has enlisted other entertainment stars, business leaders, religious institutions, and foundations. Indeed, a leading American journal of politics deemed Bono the most politically effective celebrity of all time. Always savvy about the business side of music, Bono also began nurturing his entrepreneurial instincts more aggressively. He launched a private equity firm and purchased a stake in social-networking giant Facebook. Rather than distracting him from his career as a musician, these extracurricular pursuits seem to have infused it with more energy.

We can learn a great deal from Bono's example, beginning with the fact that, paradoxically, the more focus we have, the more we need to step outside of our usual rituals and frames of reference. Changing U2's sound at the height of its fame was a risky move—not only because it had the potential to alienate fans but also because it overturned an entire approach to the craft and persona that U2 had spent years perfecting. From the hindsight of more than twenty years, it looks like a stroke of genius. My guess is that on the band's worst days at that time it felt more like a surge of insanity. At the same time, it's not as if U2 gave up making music to pursue a career in professional soccer—and therein lies another important lesson. Staying focused has a lot to do with how fresh we feel, but it doesn't necessarily entail radically altering everything about our lives. Rather, it can be quite effective to stay within our general areas of desire and expertise. We just need to step back from them often enough to notice where we're in danger of growing stale and make adjustments.

∽⟨⊙⟩∾

We live in a culture that celebrates desires and success but often skips right over the need for focus, which is, after all, the vital link that bridges them. Not surprisingly, we end up with too many unfulfilled people who sense a deeper calling but are frustrated by their inability to progress toward it. For committing ourselves to rituals, sticking with them through stretches of weakness, and finding ways to stay alive to these practices, we probably will not be rewarded with a career as remarkable as Bernardin's or the iconic status of Mother Teresa or the fabulous wealth of Bono. But those were not the ends they were chasing from the start anyway. They were far more concerned with following their desires and pushing themselves to higher and higher levels of performance—and their remarkable worldly success was a by-product of a deep commitment to their calling, as well as some luck and good timing that was beyond their control.

We can draw considerable inspiration from them. But we'll likely gain even more wisdom and encouragement from the family, friends, teachers, coaches, and clergy in our lives who model the same characteristics. This is why teachers like Barry Smith and Dick Cleary continue to matter to me a great deal. Their lessons about the value of focus still endure decades after I left their classrooms. With persistence, we can change our habits; with the potential we unlock, we can more firmly embrace our callings and show others how to do the same.

CHAPTER FIVE

Humility: Embracing
What You Don't Know

A FEW YEARS AGO MY COLLEGE ROOMMATE, Andrew, and I got together to play a little tennis—a routine enough occurrence, except for two important points. One, it was a blazing hot August afternoon in North Carolina. Two, we agreed that the loser had to pay for dinner immediately afterward. I certainly had no intention of doing that, and neither did Andrew. Ignoring the heat as best we could, we played at full steam. The match dragged on, back and forth, for about an hour. Totally intent on winning as fast as possible, I rarely bothered to sip from my bottle of Gatorade, which was warming by the minute in the scorching sun. I scratched out a victory in the first set. Then, as I had Andrew down to the final point of the match, I charged the net for an easy return shot that seemed sure to finish him off—and promptly smacked it into the tape. Everything changed from there. Andrew came back from way behind to win that set. He won the next one, too, and just like that the match was his.

As we got into our cars, he called over, "My car says it's 101 degrees out here!" Right about then, I started to feel sick. Blasting the air conditioner on the way to the restaurant didn't help, nor did gulping the preheated Gatorade. By the time we sat down in the booth for our traditional post-match meal at a nearby steak joint, I felt on the verge of vomiting. I was parched, my hands were numb, and my feet were tingling. Too weak even to sit, I stretched out flat on my back in the booth, much to the alarm of our waitress and to the great curiosity of our fellow patrons. As the minutes passed, my dinner sat completely untouched. Meanwhile, Andrew dug into his complimentary steak with gusto. "I hope I'm not having heat stroke," I moaned from beneath the table. "I hope you're not either," said Andrew, who is in fact a Harvard-trained doctor, as he took another bite. Now and then I'd lift my head long enough to see the waitress frown or a nearby diner stare for a bit. After an hour and a couple massive glasses of water, sipped fearfully through a straw, I began to rally, though not quite enough to rise from the booth seat. "Listen, man," I croaked. "I'm really sorry for making a spectacle out of us."

"Are you kidding me?" he said, pausing for a bit to savor the final bites of his free meal. "I have three little kids. I've already suffered every possible public humiliation."

It's a memory Andrew and I still get a good laugh from today. I'd probably benefit from more days like it. We usually don't stop long enough to acknowledge it, but we're always tiptoeing right along that very thin line between being in command of our powers and lying flat on our back in a restaurant, all dignity—even the slightest concern for maintaining it—completely gone. "A little humility's good for you," my dad used to say when I struck out in

Little League or failed a calculus test in high school. Even more than that, it's absolutely essential to winding our way toward and ultimately embracing our calling. As discussed in the previous two chapters, pausing to sound out our desires and making time to follow them is a vital step in discerning a vocation—so is developing the focus to screen out distractions and fight through the inertia that plagues us all.

Naming our desires and cultivating discipline are a good start. But they are not nearly enough. Why? Because it turns out that it's possible to get that far in our journey without acquiring much self-awareness—and that makes us prone to hubris, selfishness, and bad decisions. And the more passion and focus we have, without the attendant self-awareness, the more (and more serious) bad decisions we are capable of making.

There are bankers, for instance, who have a burning desire to make money. They also have the focus to work ninety hours a week and compete ferociously during every minute of it. The problems begin when desire and focus aren't held in check. That's when greed emerges. It's when the temptation to cut corners amplifies, and ambition overwhelms common sense. When I moved to central North Carolina in 1997 to start my newspaper career, Wachovia was one of the largest banks in the Southeast. Founded in Winston-Salem in the late 1800s, it had long prided itself on the "Wachovia Way," a conservative, responsible philosophy of business in an industry replete with dangerous risk takers. For generations, investors had relied on the bank for steady, if unspectacular, returns. For many residents of my community, especially retirees, Wachovia was about as safe a bet as you could make in the stock market.

The bank's executives, however, dreamed of expanding. Wall Street analysts had been saying for a long time Wachovia could grow into a major national player, but only if it started taking some chances. So, finally, it did. In 2001, the bank shocked its own workforce and home community by merging with First Union, a larger bank trying to reinvent its own brand after a series of poorly executed acquisitions. The new bank kept the name Wachovia, which suddenly ranked among the five largest financial institutions in the United States. Intent on extending its footprint even more, Wachovia bought Golden West to give it a stronger presence in California and other key markets. At the time, critics raised objections—mainly that Golden West held a lot of complicated mortgage loans that could go bad if the housing market slowed. No longer the cautious, humble bank it had once been, Wachovia brushed aside these warnings, with CEO Ken Thompson assuring shareholders "you would have to have huge unemployment and a huge downdraft in home values before this product got hit in any way."

That, of course, is exactly what happened. The subprime-mortgage crisis hammered Wachovia. Freighted with a huge portfolio of bad loans and frightened customers racing to withdraw funds, Wachovia nearly failed before the federal government stepped in to save it. In the end, Wells Fargo, which had been wary of subprime mortgages and managed its loan portfolio far more prudently, bought Wachovia for just $5.87 a share. Two years earlier at the time of the Golden West purchase, Wachovia's shares had sold for nearly $60. The impact of the collapsed stock value, particularly in North Carolina, was devastating: billions of dollars of wealth wiped out, the investment portfolios of retirees gutted, thousands of jobs lost. It was a very expensive lesson for having too little humility.

But let's not pick exclusively on bankers. Many of us, after all, egged them on by eagerly accepting loans we had little chance of repaying—a reminder that we're all prone in many ways to a lack of humility as parents, as friends, as spouses, and in every line of work. We can know exactly what we want and devise just the right means for getting there but still lack the self-awareness to see the regrettable destinations to which our choices could lead. A well-honed sense of humility—an honest acknowledgement of our many weaknesses and flaws— can make a major difference.

For Christians looking to navigate this challenge as they live out their callings, the example of Jesus can be particularly instructive. He came into this world with the mission of redeeming it. Achieving that goal in his brief lifetime was his deepest desire and one that he grasped quite early. His discipline, too, was formidable. From the start of his public ministry until the very end, he was an extraordinarily driven man, capable of performing miracles, deflecting constant attacks from his enemies, teaching, preaching, and nurturing his followers, and engaging in ceaseless prayer, all with very little rest or opportunity for renewal. I'd always assumed it was pure discipline that made it possible for him to endure the forty days of fasting in the wilderness that followed his baptism by John. The devil tested him mightily, urging him to turn stones into desperately needed food, to throw himself at the mercy of angels, to forsake God in exchange for ruling the world. Jesus was the son of God but also a man, a starving, worn-out man too long bereft of sustenance and companionship. To stave off the devil's advances under these circumstances, clearly he possessed an iron will. Or maybe there was more to it than that.

Urged to turn the stones into loaves, Jesus replies, "Man shall not live by bread alone, but by every word that proceeds from the mouth of God." When challenged to hurl himself down from the top of the temple, he says, "Again it is written, 'You shall not tempt the Lord your God.'" Finally, offered the world in exchange for his soul, Jesus responds, "Begone, Satan! For it is written, 'You shall worship the Lord your God and him only shall you serve.'"

In fending off the devil, Jesus succeeds not by sheer force of will but by making the matter more about God than about himself. Notice he never uses the words "I" or "my" once. Ultimately, Jesus' response is grounded not only in having the focus to resist temptation. It is also powerfully informed by having the self-knowledge to know where he fits in the grand scheme of things. Jesus doesn't waste time trying to formulate his own answers to the devil; he knows they wouldn't be better than the ones that scripture provides. He doesn't need to toy with the notion of being all-powerful; he's well aware that's not his role any more than it was his role to baptize his cousin John. He is in the world not to reign but to serve, not to test but to trust. That is humility at its very core. How do we develop it in service of our vocation and, even more significantly, our salvation?

The short answer: very deliberately. It's true that life is bound to bring us all our fair share of humiliations—the dressing down from a boss, the joke that no one at the party gets, the stomach bug that sends us sprinting for the bathroom. These misfortunes are typically more the exception than the rule in our daily lives, however. And that is precisely the problem. We need to pursue humility in the same way we go about eating better or exercising—through daily, intentional efforts. Three time-honored practices come to mind when I think of both my own experiences and people I've known or read about. All of these practices, by the way, are much easier said than done. First, we can work on seeing and accepting the world as it is and embracing it in joyful, hopeful ways, instead of raging in frustration when events spin out of our control. What requires more humility than that?

Second, we can spend time listening to people with whom we don't agree, who see the world and live in it differently than we do. This can be aggravating, especially as we graduate from the mixing bowl of high school and college into adulthood. There, we become increasingly free to choose the neighborhoods, friends, and media we prefer, screening out whatever annoys us. Still, every now and then, it's worth checking out a blog crammed with opinions that are the exact opposite of ours. Instead of cutting off that pesky cousin the next time he starts attacking your favorite politician, see if you can dig a little bit deeper into why he thinks that way. Perhaps we'll confirm our strong suspicions that these people are idiots, charlatans, or worse. Or maybe we'll learn we're not as smart as we thought we were. Finally, there's a lot to be said for putting ourselves, from time to time, in situations that make us uncomfortable, where our usual assumptions and talents don't serve us especially well. This is especially challenging because, as a society, we're terrified of failure. As students, we learn that an *F* is a cause for shame, not an invitation to improve. As employees, we find it's often safer to keep our heads down than propose a bold idea that might fizzle and embarrass us in front of our bosses. Rather than trying to learn from it, we attempt to avoid failure altogether and miss out on the accompanying opportunities to grow in both wisdom and humility.

When it came to seeing and accepting the world as it is and still finding reasons for faith, my Grandma Marie, born in 1900 in western Pennsylvania to Italian immigrants, left a powerful legacy. Things were never easy for her. As a child, she was shuttled among relatives when her father walked away from his family to return to Italy. At nineteen, she married my grandfather. Over the next twenty-five years, she gave birth to eleven children, all but the last of whom were born in her house. She was twenty when her oldest arrived and sixty when her youngest graduated from high school.

In between were forty grinding years of endless housework—preparing meals every day without fast food or a microwave and cleaning them up without a dishwasher. Forty years of scrubbing clothes on a washboard, of being the first to wake in a dark, freezing house to stoke the coals in the furnace. Forty years, most of them before the advent of antibiotics and vaccines, spent confronting accidents and seizures and dreaded diseases. By the time I came along as the twenty-third of twenty-six grandchildren, she was still working hard.

I vividly remember one summer visit to her house when she sweated away the afternoon cooking up a big pot of spaghetti and meatballs in her un-air-conditioned kitchen. When the meal was on the table, she escaped to the relative cool of the front porch to rest on a glider while the rest of us sat down to eat. As a kid, it didn't strike me as anything remarkable. Wasn't that what grandmothers did? Now, though, that image stands out for me as one of quiet toughness and service and love, a microcosm of how she had spent the eighty or so years that preceded it and would live out the few that were left before she died of a heart attack just short of her eighty-ninth birthday. Short, straightforward, and a little crusty, Grandma Marie projected seriousness. "Hi Mum!" my mom said once as we arrived at her house for a visit. "Do you like my new sun hat?" Grandma Marie sized up the broad-brimmed, cloth-covered accessory. "No," she declared flatly.

Like many Italians of her generation, she was never more serious than when it came to her Catholic faith. She always made it to Mass and holy days, prayed constantly, and took special pride in having a son who became a priest. In her backyard stood a statue of Mary, and religious icons adorned the house. She was steeped not in theology or the major social issues of the day but in the concrete practice of her faith—and no wonder. Catholicism helped her make sense of her hard life and gave her the sustenance to get through it gracefully. She passed it along to all of her children, including my mom, who passed it along to me and my brother. Indeed, Grandma Marie, who rarely ventured across the county line, traveled to the other side of the state at eighty years old to see me receive my First Communion. During the visit, she was out on the back porch one afternoon with my brother looking at some of his preschool work. All was well until she spotted the name of the preschool. "St. Paul's LUTHERAN CHURCH?" she yelped. My mom had some explaining to do, but my First Communion a few days later reassured Grandma Marie that our spiritual house was still in order. A number of years later at her funeral, a bishop of a Pittsburgh diocese, where my Capuchin uncle worked, delivered the homily, extolling the calling she'd found as a wife, mother, and upstanding Catholic. Everything he said made as much sense as it could to a sixteen-year-old kid. But it wasn't until I had children of my own that I really began to grasp the nature of her call, the price it exacted, and how loyally she'd honored it.

An essential element of humility is the ability to regard reality free of our egotistical tendencies and to accept it for what it is—and that's a special challenge for Christians. Many people claim to be realists, to view the world precisely as it is, and they often aren't the most pleasant company. Realism can quickly become the realm of the cynics, stoics, and fatalists among us, an arena of widespread bitterness, negativity, and regret. Have you read any of the diatribes in recent years by Christopher Hitchens, Sam Harris, and their New Atheist compatriots? They are proud realists, and they are angry.

Christians, however, claim to see the world in all its imperfection and agony and still remain hopeful and joyful. My Grandma Marie was a realist by nature and by training. She endured hardships and pain that extended well beyond the mind-boggling, day-to-day struggles of raising a large family in an era that preceded modern medicine and conveniences. During World War II, one of her oldest boys was sent straight into some of the thickest fighting on the European front. There was nothing for her to do but pray, and she did that relentlessly, marching her kids up the hill to the nearby church to do the same, braving the telegrams that came intermittently and could bring terrible news. In my uncle's case they always reported injuries he survived, but that didn't make it any easier on her.

Twenty years later, my grandfather, who owned a service station in town, was mortally wounded when a drunk driver caused a gas pump to explode and set him on fire. He somehow survived for four months before the injuries killed him. Another twenty years passed, and Grandma Marie again faced tragedy—the sudden death of her youngest son at age forty-seven. She never struck me as emotional by any means, and seeing her tears at his funeral was devastating.

Yet somehow, despite a lifetime of exhaustion, punctuated by several emotional traumas and tragedies, she lived to the end with a certain quiet joy—praising God, taking delight in her grandchildren, chuckling at our jokes and foibles. Though she's been gone more than twenty years now, her example continues to inspire. I think of this sometimes when I stagger around in the middle of the night dispensing Tylenol to my own children or rubbing a cramped leg or trying to get them out the door to school when I'm feeling too ill to stand: "How in the heck did she do this *eleven* times!"

She left us a fundamental lesson for cultivating humility that we can adopt at any age: don't spend too much time pondering God's will. Merely embrace what you have to do from one moment to the next and trust it will move you toward the person God wants you to be, even if all it seems to move you toward in the moment is frustration and despair. And that's a beautiful truth about humility—we don't have to go out of our way to develop it.

Every instant of every day is in fact an invitation to humble ourselves. We can refrain from blasting the horn at someone who cuts us off in traffic on the way to work. We can resist the temptation to have the last word in a spat with our spouse. We can get dinner on the table when we'd rather be taking a nap. But it's not easy; sometimes, it seems we're hardwired for selfishness.

From the moment of our birth, when we emerge demanding food from our mothers, we are consumed by wanting. Getting what we want only makes us want more and increases our expectation that we'll get it. Our impatience and frustration with anything that stands in the way of our wants increases in direct proportion to our hunger. We become more and more convinced that we can create exactly the lives we want, and we can do it by exerting control over our environment.

We are not likely, for example, to spend much time with people who challenge our most treasured assumptions, people with whom we rarely see eye to eye. Doing so is a startling notion for modern-day Americans. The fragmentation of media makes it easy to spend time listening exclusively to news and commentary with which we wholeheartedly agree. Political conservatives can retreat to their private world of conservative talk shows, television channels, websites and magazines. Liberals can do the same—and both sides increasingly do. That's not surprising, of course. It's comforting to hole up in an echo chamber that reaffirms the rightness of our own ideas, shields us from threats, and rarely challenges us to think or act in new ways. It's a great way to build up our own self-regard. Sadly, it doesn't do much at all for our sense of humility.

Henri Matisse, the wordly, atheistic avant-garde genius who, along with Picasso, dominated the art world for the first half of the twentieth century, has much to teach us in this regard. Like many of the groundbreaking artists of his time, Matisse, though baptized a Roman Catholic, didn't have much use for religion. Tied as it was to tradition, authority, and the status quo—all things he and his peers wished mightily to shatter—the faith was something he did not wish to embrace. He and his friend and great rival, Pablo Picasso, devoted their lives instead to revolutionizing the art world, ushering in a modern era of color, abstraction, and vivid expression.

Right up until his death in 1954 at age eighty-four, Matisse was highly controversial with fellow artists, critics, and the general public, in large part because he was always several steps ahead of his contemporaries, stretching the very definition of art with his paintings, sculptures, and cutouts. Perhaps none of his creations pushed the limits more than his Chapelle du Rosaire, or Chapel of the Rosary, in the south of France. Regarded by Matisse himself as his masterpiece, the small Catholic chapel, which he designed for a group of Dominican nuns, is now regarded among the great religious buildings of the twentieth century. How it came to be is a study in vocation and the power of humility.

Beset with abdominal cancer in 1941, Matisse endured devastating operations that nearly killed him and confined him to a wheelchair for the rest of his life. Determined to continue his work, he advertised for a nurse who could also double as a model for his art. A young woman named Monique Bourgeois won the job. She worked closely with him before joining a Dominican convent in Vence in 1943 as Sr. Jacques Marie.

Matisse eventually bought a house nearby Sr. Jacques Marie. She visited him there and mentioned that her Dominican sisters wanted to build a new chapel. Would Matisse be interested in helping design it? He'd never done a project like it, but, ever-ambitious, he always looked for opportunities to break new artistic ground. In 1947, he agreed to work on the chapel. So began his immersion into the world of Catholicism, through which this longtime atheist and perceived enemy of faith kept regular company with priests and nuns, scandalizing both the anti-Catholic art world and the Catholic hierarchy.

Had Matisse behaved with the black-and-white rigidness many of our political pundits encourage today, the project never would have gotten started at all. Imagine for a moment: Matisse was not a fan of the Church. Now all of a sudden his nurse and artistic collaborator was abandoning him for a convent? Her choice must have baffled if not outright infuriated him. Still, he stayed open to this relationship and respectful of his young assistant's own calling. That act of humility changed both of their lives.

Working feverishly with Sr. Jacques Marie and Br. Louis Bertrand Rayssiguier, a modern-art enthusiast and recent graduate of the Sorbonne, Matisse meticulously planned out every minute detail of the chapel, from its outward design all the way down to the vestments to be worn there by priests. Increasingly, he also bankrolled its design and construction. Approaching eighty years old and in chronically bad health, he saw the chapel as his last big chance to do something great—and he faced plenty of obstacles to its completion.

"The scheme was crazily impractical," Matisse biographer Hilary Spurling writes. "Matisse might be a major figure on the international stage, but his fame cut no ice with the lower echelons of the Roman Catholic Church."[1] More horrifying yet was his penchant for drawing nudes. Even the nuns for whom he wished to build the chapel mocked his modernist plans for it. The project was saved when Fr.

Marie-Alain Courturier, a key figure in France's fight over the future of religious art, took an interest and quickly gained all the necessary Church approvals to proceed with the chapel. Still, the struggle to finish it took a toll, from Matisse's marathon work sessions to Br. Rayssiguier's tortured attempts to keep all parties appeased. Rayssiguier tried to quit, but Matisse won him over with a sincere, humble appeal. "I am an invalid, even if I do my best to disguise it," Matisse begged him. "I need a second-in-command; I can do nothing without you."[2]

The chapel was consecrated in June 1951, after four years of intense effort. By then the nuns were its biggest champions, dazzled by its elaborate stained-glass windows, huge black-line wall drawings, and stark white interior. In the words of art critic Susan Sternau, "An atmosphere of spirituality is created by the colored light that floods into the chapel from the many windows and reflects off the tile walls and floor. Matisse's elegant hand is also visible in the altar and its furniture, the crucifix, chasubles, and various other details."[3] Matisse was too ill to attend the consecration but received praise from a bishop, who declared, "The human author of all that we see here is a man of genius who, all his life, worked, searched, strained himself, in a long and bitter struggle, to draw near the truth and the light."[4]

Matisse never formally rejoined the Church, but his remarkable willingness to steep himself in its traditions, cultivate deep friendships with its adherents, and open himself to a new kind of spirituality clearly had a powerful impact on him. Even with his body badly failing him, Matisse's creative powers blossomed anew in the few years he had left after finishing the chapel. At an age when many people find their skills to have long ago withered, Matisse created some of his most enduring works of art. He had the humility to surround himself with contrary people and ideas that might have seriously threatened the self-identity of a lesser man—and he moved that much deeper into his calling as a result.

A key reason Matisse succeeded not only in tolerating but also in working with and learning from people very different from him was that he was pursuing a higher goal—in this case, the completion of a highly ambitious work of art—and he wouldn't let anything get in the way. Practicing humility in this instance wasn't merely an isolated exercise in self-improvement; it was central to achieving the outcomes he wanted. We might then say, "Well, he was probably being humble for what were ultimately selfish reasons." Maybe. But, in doing so, he also made the world around him a better place—by creating an enduring masterpiece, by offering inspiration to the nuns of Vence and generations of spiritual seekers, and by showing what we're capable of accomplishing even at advanced ages. We, too, might benefit from imagining results we'd like to see and opening ourselves up to unfamiliar ideas and jarring relationships to realize them. We could start right now in our own families.

Paying respect to our parents and always seeking to learn from them is a noble goal—and one also required of us by the Ten Commandments. Making that happen often requires some humility—a willingness to overlook an insult or a personality quirk, or to coexist with baffling political notions and different tastes. Like Matisse, we're trying to build something lasting—a relationship we can enjoy more now and look to later on for wisdom and comfort. We won't get too far on that journey if our pride keeps getting in the way. So, when Mom makes a catty remark about your daughter's haircut or Dad reminds you how you always screw up your tax returns, try to fake humility for a while, to bite your lip and tell yourself the end of a deeper connection will eventually justify the means. In doing so, we'll inch a little closer toward strong relationships and also make humility a little more of a habit.

Fully embracing the demands and joys of our daily existence, as Grandma Marie did, and opening ourselves to unfamiliar people and ideas, as did Matisse, offer two paths for growing in humility. Putting ourselves in situations in which we are no longer the experts, in which the many weaknesses we've kept hidden from ourselves might be exposed, provides a third way. When we're skilled at something, whether it's running a household or putting a ball in a hoop or cutting out tumors, we can become a little too impressed with ourselves. We quickly forget the enormous multitude of things at which we have absolutely no skill at all. When we've worked hard and also been a little lucky and created a fairly predictable, secure life for ourselves, we can become a little too complacent. To quote Jesuit priest Walter Ciszek: "We all too easily come to equate being comfortable with a sense of well-being, to seek our comfort solely in the sense of being comfortable. Friends and possessions surround us, one day is followed by the next, good health and happiness for the most part are ours."[5] It's a pleasant life. Who, after all, wouldn't want that? It's also fertile ground for pride to take root. Ciszek reminds us that God will find ways to break through that routine and make us uncomfortable again for our own good. But we don't need to wait to be dragged into those moments of vulnerability and serious uncertainty. We can, like St. Francis of Assisi, go out looking for them ourselves.

If you're like me, you might recall St. Francis rather benignly, as a callow youth who walked away from great wealth, as a cheerful advocate for peace, as a lover of animals great and small. He was indeed all of these things. It wasn't until quite recently, however, when a Franciscan priest gave me a copy of Markus Hofer's *Francis for Men*, that I better understood the nature of his evolution from playboy to saint. It goes something like this. After spending a hard year as a prisoner of war in his early twenties, Francis, the son of a rich merchant, soured a bit on the glories of war and the pursuit of knighthood, to which many well-to-do young men of his age aspired. Still, when a new military campaign presented itself, he outfitted himself in the best armor money could buy and prepared himself for the journey. But the night before he was to set off for the fight, he rather inexplicably gave away his suit of armor to a poor knight who couldn't afford it, and went home to Assisi instead. There he resumed his work at his father's firm and his well-established role among friends as the life of the party. Sometime later, he made a pilgrimage to Rome, where he spontaneously gave away all his silver coins at the tombs of the apostles. Proceeding outside, he spotted a beggar and traded his own designer clothes for the beggar's rags. He took a short turn at begging, asked for his clothes back, and went on his way.

Francis wasn't afraid to make a fool of himself in his experiments with faith. He gladly put himself in situations in which his inherited wealth, fine education, and knowledge of business didn't really help, and in which he was almost certain to draw ridicule from friends and family.

How willing are we to do the same? It's much safer never to trade our clothes at all. Still, as Hofer writes, poverty was a notion "he cultivated from the safe distance of a bourgeois existence. He was still the well-off almsgiver with the emotional backup of his protected existence."[6] All that changed one day in the valley below Assisi.

Coming upon a leper, whose foul odors typically sickened him, Francis didn't hold his nose this time. Instead, shockingly and rather dangerously for his own health, he kissed the leper's hand. He then went even a step farther, embracing him for the kiss of peace. From that moment, Francis was a changed man. I had previously assumed that in that moment he'd also found his calling. Actually, all he'd found at that point was the humility needed to enter into it. And that's no small thing. But he was still a long way from becoming the saint who permanently altered Catholic perceptions of spirituality and founded one of the most influential orders in the history of the Church. Right there, at the very beginning, he was humble and confused. He intuited a great destiny for himself but didn't know what it was. As Hofer writes, "The path lay before him but he did not have much more than a vague orientation. There was more fog than clarity, more bewilderment than signposts."[7]

Francis wandered around outside the city. He lived in a cave for a month, hiding from family members who were certain he'd lost his mind. He began to rebuild a ruined chapel, using the proceeds from his own sales of his father's fabrics. That, of course, led to a famous confrontation with his father. Summoned to the bishop's palace, Francis was ordered to return the money he'd taken. Not stopping there, he stripped off his clothes and gave them to his father as well. He left the palace naked and pub-licly renounced his father in favor of God. From there, he embarked on the life of poverty, service, and prayer for which he became legendary.

Francis's calling unfolded slowly and quite painfully at times, but he was on the right track. In all likelihood, he would never have stumbled upon it at all without the humility and self-awareness he gained from thrusting him-self into unfamiliar situations—with the poor knight, the Roman beggar, the leper, and finally his father—that jolted him out of his comfort zone and opened up new realms of possibility.

It's worth noting that St. Francis's example is inspir-ing but also extreme. Many of us are not in a position to chuck everything we've known and start anew. We have mortgages to pay, children to raise, parents who depend on us. Maybe we already do find considerable meaning in our lives and don't want to upend them entirely in service of humility. That's fine. In fact, that pretty much describes my life. We should recognize, though, that St. Francis's challenge remains valid. Interacting with people with whom we don't see eye to eye, as Matisse modeled for us, isn't easy. St. Francis calls us to push ahead even farther by stepping well outside our comfort zones and exposing ourselves willingly to fear and the very real possibility of failure.

The ways in which we might step outside our com-fort zone are as vast as the number of individuals in the world—we all have our own personal terrors, after all. Many people have a deep-seated fear of death and dying. They don't want to read about it or talk about it or, especially, be around it. For them, taking up St. Francis's challenge might mean volunteering to work a few hours a week in a hospital or nursing home. Others might have a substantial, but mostly uncultivated, talent in art or math or ministry, but they're not using it because they started down a different career path that didn't draw on those passions. Now, with mortgages, families, and professional identities to worry about, it's too frightening to contemplate veering in another direction, even if it would be far more fulfilling. For those folks, finding ways to switch careers, or take small, positive steps in that direction, could be their equivalent of acting on St. Francis's call. Whatever we choose to do, it doesn't need to be all-consuming. But we need to create space in our lives, in healthy, directed ways, for those things that make us uneasy and bring fear close to the surface.

My boss, a retired US Navy admiral, likes to say leadership is like a muscle; the more you exercise it, the stronger you get. The same might be said of humility. Our goal in pursuing this quality is not to mold ourselves into meek, retreating people firmly convinced of our own worthlessness. On the contrary, finding and fulfilling our vocations, as the many examples in this book suggest, requires confidence, toughness, and ambition. We don't sacrifice those traits—indeed, we enhance them—when we take on the hard work of embracing the twists and turns of our daily lives and learning to accept where our influence ends and God's begins. Paradoxically, we grow wiser by investing time with people and ideas from which we'd much sooner just walk away. We increase our strength by routinely entering into circumstances that make us uncomfortable. Humility, fortunately for the vast majority of us, doesn't necessitate the pursuit of something grand. Most of us will not raise eleven children or create a critically acclaimed chapel or achieve sainthood. Instead, we're bound to live out St. Thérèse of Lisieux's "Little Way"—doing what we need to do each day faithfully in service of God. We bear the inevitable disappointments and frustrations—the screaming children, the missed promotion, the lost friendship. We give thanks for the little moments of grace—the word of encouragement from a colleague, a baby's nap that goes fifteen minutes longer than expected, the gentle hoot of an owl in the woods.

As author Robert Ellsberg explains, St. Thérèse "believed that this way might transform any situation into a profound arena for holiness, and one that might thus, through the effect of subtle ripples, make a significant contribution to transforming the world."[8] It also simply makes a lot of sense to be humble in our pursuit of humility, to edge toward our callings with small steps.

When I started writing essays about faith, shortly after my thirtieth birthday, I dreamed of getting published right away in all the big Catholic magazines. How could they not like my work? How far could my ambition take me? Then the rejections, some of which came with notes enumerating precisely what they didn't like, started rolling in. Stung and discouraged, I stopped trying altogether for a year or two. Then, emboldened once again, I set a small goal of getting an essay published in my diocesan newspaper. It took a little work, but it finally happened. Over time came some more essays that ended up in bigger publications. Humility, I've found, can help us enormously in growing into vocations. Along the way, we might surprise ourselves. We might just find out we're capable of far more than we thought.

CHAPTER SIX

Community: Getting
Outside of Yourself

NEAR THE END OF MY FRESHMAN YEAR AT DUKE IN
1992, something happened that shocked the campus community: the university announced a speaker for that
spring's commencement ceremony whom most of us
didn't recognize. Everyone expected another celebrity
along the lines of television journalists Tom Brokaw and
Ted Koppel or cartoonist Garry Trudeau, who had all pre-
sided over recent graduation exercises. Instead, that year's
senior class would hear from someone named Marian
Wright Edelman, president of something called the Children's Defense Fund. Around campus and in the student
newspaper, the reaction went something like this: Who in
the world is she? And why aren't we hearing from some
really famous person who has made a ton of money?

If Edelman were aware of the criticism, it probably
would have amused her. She had, after all, spent her entire
career putting urgent causes—rather than herself—in the
limelight. Having grown up in the segregated South as

a Baptist minister's daughter, she graduated from Yale Law School in 1963 and immediately thrust herself into the heart of the civil rights struggle. She worked for the NAACP Legal and Defense Fund in New York and then took the fight to Mississippi, where she became the first black woman admitted to the state bar. Later, she coordinated Martin Luther King Jr.'s Poor People's Campaign. She and her husband, Peter Edelman, an assistant to Robert F. Kennedy, met while visiting Mississippi's Delta slums and ultimately had three children. And it was children that became the heart of Edelman's work. In 1973, she founded the Children's Defense Fund to lead advocacy and research on behalf of disadvantaged youngsters across the United States. In the decades since, her nonprofit has taken the plight of suffering children to policymakers and the public and spearheaded the development of numerous programs that have come to their aid. Her groundbreaking work has won her many awards, including the Presidential Medal of Freedom.

Certainly, much of her success is rooted in the three vocational practices we have covered so far. Edelman had a burning desire, even as a small child, to help people—especially those struggling with discrimination. So it was not surprising that social justice became a core of her calling. She was very focused as well—a top student who found ways to balance a highly productive career as a lawyer, activist, writer and executive with the demands of marriage and motherhood. She was also humble—always willing to learn, capable of keeping her ego in check, undeterred when her pleas on behalf of children were ignored. What has really made Edelman stand out, however, has been her enthusiastic embrace of community.

Left to her own devices, there's a good chance Edelman would have taken her desires, focus, and humility and carved out a successful career as an academic. And there wouldn't have been anything wrong with that at all—except regret later for not having honored other notions bubbling up inside her. Looking at the suffering around her in an era of frightening racism, poverty, and hopelessness for minorities in America, she concluded that pursuing her own private interests wasn't enough. "I hadn't planned on going to law school. I wanted to study nineteenth-century Russian literature," Edelman told *US News & World Report.* "But I got mad one day when I went down to the NAACP and saw all these people who didn't have lawyers. The white lawyers wouldn't take cases. So I applied to law school—hated it, but I stayed because it was the right tool then." That decision set the tone for the rest of her life. Her calling would be shaped not just by what she wanted—but also by what people around her needed.

It is tempting, especially among Americans who greatly value individualism, to regard calling as a private matter that is primarily about personal growth. Certainly it is a highly personal matter. No two people have precisely the same callings, and, ultimately, no one else can decide for us what our callings are. Cultivating desires, focus, and humility requires a good deal of inner work that no one else can do for us. It's logical, if incorrect, to give ourselves the lion's share of the credit as we begin to embrace our purpose and reap the rewards. After all, we really sweated to get there! The reality is, however, we are helped along by others at every stage of the journey. Without Dr. Fowlie, I might still be in the wilderness. Without my wife, Dawn, my awareness would be far more limited. Teachers I was fortunate to have from grade school onward made clear my strongest desires involved writing. Becoming a father radically improved my focus. It was also humbling, despite the pride I take in my independence, to find I couldn't cope with my anxiety disorder alone. Doctors, friends, and family members made a huge difference.

Without question, there exists a dimension of community to our callings that is especially incumbent upon Christians to recognize—and that Marian Wright Edelman grasped early in her life. As St. Paul reminds us in Romans 12, "for as in one body we have many members, and all the members do not have the same function, so we, though many, are one body in Christ, and individually members of one another." In terms of calling, his words have serious implications. Most significantly, an overriding sense of community is inherent to Christianity, which cannot thrive without it. The individual callings of Christians are unique but intended to contribute collectively to the betterment of this community of faith.

To say Christians are "individually members of one another," from the standpoint of calling, means they have a real stake not only in the development of their own callings but in the progress their fellow Christians make as well. They have a responsibility to offer guidance and support to their brothers and sisters in discerning their gifts and purpose—and are equally compelled to enlist them in sounding out and embracing their own calls. If that work is not done in its entirety, individual Christians will not live up to their full potential, and the entire community suffers.

To engage fully in our callings, we need to be challenged from time to time. If we are not, then sadly, past a certain point, we're not too well positioned to either accept a challenge or even to challenge ourselves. As we often say at the leadership institute where I work, we are the worst judges of our own strengths and weaknesses. The only way to get a real reading on what we do well and where we need to improve is to ask somebody else, or preferably many other people. That's where community comes in— and where it's worth reflecting on the example of Dr. Erica Brown.

A Jewish writer and educator in Washington, DC, Brown was the subject of a thought-provoking column by David Brooks of the *New York Times*. In a piece titled "The Arduous Community," Brooks explored why high-achieving Beltway professionals are lining up for Brown's Torah study groups and adult education classes on Jewish thought.

For Brown, Jewish learning is more about fomenting struggle than creating an unearned sense of peace in her classroom. Her goal is not to make her students feel better. She wants them to feel uncomfortable. So she routinely pushes them on points of morality that they (and most of us) would rather not ponder too much. Brooks paraphrases her this way: "No, serving the poor for a few days a year isn't enough. Yes, it is necessary to expose a friend's adultery because his marriage is more important than your friendship." Brown stands out, Brooks says, because of "her ability to undermine the egos of the successful at the same time that she lovingly helps them build better lives. She offers a path out of the tyranny of the perpetually open mind by presenting authoritative traditions and teachings. Most educational institutions emphasize individual advancement. Brown nurtures the community and the group."[1]

In one of her "Weekly Jewish Wisdom" columns, Brown offers up this quote from Rabbi Haim ben Attar, an eighteenth-century intellectual: "Torah can be observed communally—by the people as a whole, each individual deriving benefit from the observance of one's neighbor and each individual's performance complementing that of the other." As Brown explains, there are 613 commandments, and it's virtually impossible for all of them to be observed by any individual Jew. Some apply only to those who live in Israel, some are specifically for priests, and others depend on circumstance. "Since no one person can observe all of the commandments together, the complete observance of the Torah requires all Jews as a whole to value the input of each other into Jewish life," Brown writes. "This seems so obvious, but in real life, nothing could be more of a challenge for Jewish life today."[2] As Brown explains, valuing the input of fellow Jews is complicated by the fact that Judaism means many different things to different Jews. Some stress religious observance, others emphasize culture, still others care most about serving their community through professional work or board service. But by isolating themselves from elements of Judaism that are unfamiliar or don't appeal as much, they limit the extent to which they can respond to and embrace their callings as modern-day Jews.

Precisely the same can be said, of course, about Christians, who are too often bitterly divided by doctrine, scripture, politics, and the mechanics of day-to-day spiritual practice. Brown writes, "One of the only ways that we will find unity amid diversity is to expose ourselves to experiences of Judaism that are unlike those we have ever had, that give value to expressions of Judaism that are unlike those of our own."³ The word "Christianity" could be inserted quite easily for "Judaism." For those of us in pursuit of callings, regardless of religious affiliation, we might also substitute "community" in the same spot. Calling, to paraphrase Rabbi Attar, can be observed communally—in fact, it must be if we are committed to remaining grounded and continuing to learn. What does this look like in practice? We can start by observing the callings of family and friends and doing what we can to support them. This is a challenge in a couple of ways. It requires not only taking the focus off ourselves and our own obsessions for a bit but also really trying to immerse ourselves in the mind and viewpoints of somebody else. That is never easy, but doing the work will almost certainly strengthen our relationships and give us new insights into the people who matter most to us.

⚭

As crucial as challenges are in discerning a call, inspiration is also vital for keeping up our spirits and commitment on the lengthy, hard, distraction-filled trek toward living out our purpose. Here again, community matters. Over the long haul, how much success will we really have trying to inspire ourselves, even if we are exceptionally self-motivated? Probably about as much success as we'll have accurately identifying what other people think of us without actually asking them. To stay fresh, even thoroughbred introverts like me need to spend time around people and organizations that rouse our passions.

This book began with a reflection on the former Duke basketball star, Bobby Hurley, whose struggles and triumphs over the past two decades prompted me to think harder about the nature and direction of my own calling. It turns out, however, that while both Hurley and I were circling around in the wilderness for a good chunk of our post-Duke years, his father Bob Hurley Sr., was living out a full-fledged calling from which we can all learn. His story seems unlikely to have unfolded as it has, however, without the deep and lasting inspiration provided by his home community of Jersey City, New Jersey.

Bob Hurley Sr. has served as head coach of St. Anthony High School's basketball team for nearly forty years. With an enrollment of fewer than three hundred students, most of them from low-income backgrounds, the Jersey City Catholic school runs an annual deficit of more than $1 million and doesn't even have its own gymnasium. Yet, Hurley has molded the boys' basketball team there into arguably the most powerful in the entire nation. One of just three high school coaches to be inducted into the national Basketball Hall of Fame, Hurley has guided the school to more than a thousand victories, twenty-six state championships, and four national championships. For the past seventeen years, every one of his players has been admitted to college. And over those four decades, Hurley has never even been a full-time employee of the school. A probation officer who later worked for the Jersey City Recreation Department, Hurley has coached at St. Anthony in his spare time, never earning more than $9,000 a year for his efforts.

Certainly, Hurley has been an inspiration to St. Anthony High School and the entire Jersey City community. He has coached hundreds of young men and permanently changed many of their lives for the better with his attention and mentorship, which continues long after they have graduated. Having been featured in the bestselling book

The Miracle of St. Anthony and the documentary film "The Street Stops Here," Hurley has attracted national attention and resources to a tiny Catholic school that otherwise would have closed long ago. Indeed, the school's current principal says that Hurley's relentless efforts to raise money through speaking engagements, basketball camps, and funding campaigns is about all that stands between the school and financial ruin. With Hurley now in his mid-sixties, the St. Anthony community is surely asking itself an uncomfortable question: How much longer will he stay—and what happens to our school when he leaves? It's also natural to ask a question even more fundamental than that: Why has he stayed so long in the first place?

Over the years, Hurley has had numerous opportunities to coach at the college level, fielding job offers that came with plenty of prestige and salaries far in excess of $9,000 annually. Yet, he has rejected all of them. That has meant leaving a fortune on the table, scraping by in worn-out facilities, and fighting to save a school that is perpetually on the verge of shutting down. Hurley could have chosen a much easier life long ago, and who would have blamed him for it? Still, the man who has inspired a city with his intense, hard-nosed coaching style draws tremendous inspiration from the St. Anthony community itself—and that seems to be the primary reason he stays.

Asked about his extraordinary loyalty in an era when even high school coaches bounce from job to job, Hurley put it this way: "Some people may just say I was never very ambitious. But I think that my wife and I found that over the years we just found so many kids that were here, that when they came into school you saw something in them, this potential, and you wanted to see it out. And then four years would go by and then there's another kid in there some place—freshman, sophomore—then eight years have gone by and all of a sudden you've got twenty years in." It's a progression that has by now consumed his entire adult life—and he doesn't regret a moment of it. "I think I'm where I'm supposed to be," Hurley says. "I think I'm good with this age, and I'm good with city kids because I was a city kid."[4] He is, in other words, inextricably linked with his community—his players, the school, and the city itself. The energy he draws from those ties fuels a passion for coaching and molding young men that's as intense now as it was forty years ago.

Hurley's story raises a tricky subject that deserves serious attention—the tensions between calling and income. Ideally, we would all find jobs that provide meaningful work and pay well. Sadly, many Americans are struggling to find any job at all these days. And, even if they are fortunate enough to land a prestigious one, there's often an inverse relationship between meaning and money. Growing up, many of us are encouraged to pursue degrees that lead to the big bucks—law, medicine, engineering, investment banking, and management consulting to name a few. But we're not as well schooled in the dirty secret of these jobs—they often entail back-breaking hours that suck the joy out of life and take a real toll on marriages and families.

Even in this era of recession, there are a lot of people out there making a lot of money and feeling miserable about their lives anyway. This isn't to say, of course, that we can't love our work and make a ton of cash at the same time. We all know people who thoroughly enjoy their work and are compensated well for it. Most of us, however, will not find ourselves in jobs that satisfy our souls and also fund regular excursions to the Caribbean. As that reality sets in, we might feel bitter or pine for something more lucrative or spend money that we don't have on nice things we don't really need.

Hurley's example reminds us of a couple crucial points. First, beyond providing food, shelter, and a reasonable quality of life for our families, money does not constitute a core element of calling. If we make earning it our primary objective, we will almost certainly end up unfulfilled in the long run. It's far more important that we find some sense of meaning or calling in what we do every day, that we are engaged in a community that challenges and inspires us. In devoting themselves to an extended family of teenage boys and a struggling Catholic school, Bob Hurley and his wife, who is also an integral part of the basketball program at St. Anthony, have chosen to live far more modestly than they might have. But the Hurleys know that's the price of a calling that rewards them in ways money never would.

Second, Hurley demonstrates a truth that eluded me for a long time—our day jobs and callings are not necessarily one and the same. Remember, Hurley supported his family by working as a probation officer. Coaching at St. Anthony, for which he is barely paid anything, is more of a ministry than a job. Yet, that work, along with his close-knit family, is clearly the part of his life in which he takes the most pride—and for which he will be remembered by everyone else. Our callings do not always emerge from the most obvious places.

Community is essential for challenging and inspiring us in pursuit of our callings—and prompting us to do the same for others. But, over the long haul, how do we keep the momentum going? How do we follow the path of Bob

Hurley, who was still just hitting his stride as a coach, mentor, and role model for disadvantaged kids in his mid forties, instead of the trail blazed by many of us, who find ourselves increasingly burned out and disenchanted at the same age? Several factors, of course, are at play, and it would be impossible and wrong to boil it all down to just one. A fundamental difference, however, between Hurley and many other people is that he enmeshed himself so deeply in the St. Anthony community that it has helped him through times of frustration and difficulty—of which there have been and continue to be many. Challenge and inspiration matter greatly, but, perhaps even more significantly, community also carries the power to sustain us.

◦◦◦

As a young newspaper reporter, I was once assigned to cover an appearance at Wake Forest University by Fr. Francis Kline, a Trappist monk. I arrived early to the classroom, where about fifteen freshmen were chattering excitedly about weekend plans for concerts and parties. Kline, the abbot of Mepkin Abbey near Charleston, South Carolina, came in and sat down and spent the next forty-five minutes explaining the rituals of monastic life. The monks woke up every day at 3:00 a.m., he said, gathered seven times a day in the abbey chapel for prayers, ate small vegetarian meals, spent their days running the monastery's egg farm, and turned out the lights at 8:00 p.m. And that's what they did—day after day, year after year, decade after decade. The schedule never changed, and the monks never left the monastery grounds unless there was an extremely compelling reason, like a doctor's appointment. The vibrant eighteen-year-olds in the classroom didn't quite know what to make of it. They were curious, respectful, intrigued. But this question was also written plainly on their faces: Is it just me, or does this all sound a little crazy?

I'd have probably thought the same thing if I hadn't already made a couple of retreats to Mepkin. The first of them, during my senior year at Duke, was one of the more disorienting experiences of my life. Determined to get the full flavor of monastic life, my friends and I arrived on a Friday afternoon and carefully followed the prescribed schedule until Monday morning. In theory, rising at 3:00 a.m. is not difficult if you go to sleep at 8:00 p.m. If, on the other hand, you're twenty-two, accustomed to staying up past midnight, and can't fall asleep until then, it starts to become a problem. Our grand experiment ended Monday morning with a buddy shaking me out of sleep and gesticulating wildly.

"What the heck is going on?" I muttered, bleary-eyed, only to be met with more frantic hand motions. "Can you just tell me what the problem is!" I nearly shouted—and then realized that he was still dutifully obeying the daily Great Silence, during which not a word was to be spoken. It had begun about twelve hours before, after Compline (the closing prayer of the previous day), and was in effect until the end of Lauds (the morning prayer), which was about to begin in five minutes! Rounding up another friend, who was in a nearby room, with more furious, wordless flailing of the arms, we raced from our rooms to the chapel, which was about a half mile away. We rushed in, out of breath and slightly late, as one of the monks waved us into our seats in the choir.

On the drive back to North Carolina, half out of our minds from sleep deprivation and lack of red meat, we debated what we'd just experienced. Reengaging with the Church as I was at that time after my overdose of Albert Camus, I'd found the whole weekend transfixing. The remarkable mindfulness of the monks and their astonishing discipline and sense of purpose made a powerful impression. To me at least, these things justified their unconventional lives. They seemed very happy about it, and I was glad someone was going about the business of praising God while the rest of us proceeded with our worldly lives. Brian, an engineer with the requisite analytical mind, wasn't so easily swayed. He too admired the holiness and focus of the monks. But, given all the illness, poverty, and crime in our society, he couldn't help but wonder if the monks wouldn't do more good outside the monastery walls, assisting people with life-threatening problems. What were they really accomplishing? My answer, then as now and straight from the heart of an impractical English major, is that they are doing what they are called to do.

Even if we don't ever fully buy into the monastic way of life, we can still learn from it—and monasteries, if nothing else, show us the power of community in sustaining a call. Monks, to be sure, lead lives of considerable sacrifice. Their meals are brief and modest. They must wake up at the very time when their natural sleep cycles are deepest. They leave behind cherished family and friends from the outside world and eschew personal possessions. They commit themselves to staying in one place for the rest of their lives. But their biggest challenge of all is knowing this routine and loss of freedom will never change, and staying alive to their call anyway.

Monks, just like the rest of us, are prone to restlessness, boredom, and mild depression, known in monastic parlance as "acedia" or "the noonday devil." As Michael Downey writes in *Trappist*, "It is at this very point that we look for distraction. This is the moment when we crave diversion, anything to break out of the routine. In the ache of the ordinary, the monk's mind may wander, and he may wonder: Will there ever be just one Friday when it's not tomato soup and cheese sandwiches for supper? What's the point of this life?"[5]

Hermits—contemplative Christians who live alone rather than in community—might have the strength to dismiss such doubts and spiritual ennui on their own. Even in the rarefied world of elite spiritual practice, however, there are not many hermits—and there's good reason for that. In the moments of trial we all face in the everyday world, companions are an important source of inspiration, solace, and hope. In navigating a monastic career that could cover six or seven decades, they are, for most contemplatives, indispensable.

There's the simple matter of encouragement, for one thing. On a day when a particular monk is feeling down, and those days are inevitable, he will encounter another monk who provides a positive word or, perhaps even saying nothing, goes about the business of washing the pots and pans from breakfast cheerfully and purposefully. At a deeper level, there are the enduring bonds that come from getting to know fellow monks extremely well. When I visited Holy Cross Abbey in Berryville, Virginia in 2010, guest master Daniel DeVoe told me "anytime you get put together with fifteen or twenty people you don't know, you'll find things about them that are objectionable, and they'll find them about you." The trick, he said, is learning to appreciate the strengths of others, to give them the

benefit of the doubt, to acknowledge your own shortcom-
ings, and work to fix them. That's easier said than done.
But when it's done right, trust—that ancient glue of monastic life—results, helping each individual monk live more
fully in community.

Monasteries, in fact, succeed only when trust and self-
sacrifice take precedence, when monks set aside personal
plans and ambitions for the greater good. They commit
to a daily, unending exercise in probing their flaws and
coming to terms with their own insignificance. This adds
up to a perpetual assault on pride, and it starts with quiet-
ing down and listening to what their brothers have to say.
"We're all so impressed by what we know," DeVoe said.

But rather than overestimating our own abilities, real
knowledge comes from paying attention to those around
us. Monks have a longstanding tradition of turning to
spiritual directors for guidance in the contemplative life.
The feedback they get gives them a better sense of their
strengths and weaknesses and serves as a spark for change.
"You learn things about yourself that you wouldn't know
otherwise," DeVoe said. Perhaps most fundamentally of
all, monks literally would not be able to live their callings
outside of a community. Running a monastery is hard
work. They have to be self-sustaining financially, which,
in the case of Holy Cross Abbey, means keeping a bakery
running daily. Meals have to be cooked, the grounds kept,
visitors greeted, administrative details tackled. The job is
bigger than what any individual monk can manage. Shar-
ing his call intimately with a larger community makes possible its fulfillment.

"Monasticism is nothing more or less than living
the gospel in a radical way," Michael Downey writes in

Trappist.[6] It is a profoundly countercultural movement that challenges the prevailing definitions of success in America today more than it ever has—with regard to status, money, possessions, consumption, rootedness, and distraction. Indeed, it is so countercultural that even the monks themselves are bound to ask now and then if they are not simply wasting their time, not to mention their lives. Without the presence of their brothers and a larger, supportive community in such times of doubt, it unquestionably would be harder to stay alive to their highly unusual call. Then again, a belief that calling should be the primary driver of our daily decisions and the guiding light of our long-term pursuits—that our integrity and happiness rest on more than the sum of our worldly achievements and the well-reasoned, logical pursuit of them—also slices hard against the grain of modern life. Most of us will not reject our consumer society as radically as monks. But making choices in service of a larger purpose, rather than in lockstep with convention, is a countercultural response too. To follow our callings wholeheartedly is to live in the spirit of the monk, provided we proceed in the spirit of community.

How do we deliberately tap into the sustaining power of community in our own lives? It's important to recognize that if even monks—elite athletes of purpose and vocation—are subject to acedia, the rest of us could really get into trouble with it. So we should accept the inevitable: we will all struggle with boredom, listlessness, and distraction to at least some degree at every stage of our lives, no matter how deeply engaged we are with our calls. There's no way to avoid it; the key is being prepared for it and knowing how to work through it.

The example of the Trappist monks reminds us that immersing ourselves in community must be at the core of our response. Some concrete implications follow. First, we need to allow our family and friends to help us by letting them into our lives. Despite the fact that I've laid bare a very painful period of my life in the opening chapters of this book, I'm by nature an introvert and a very private person. It's rare that I'll share my complete thoughts on a situation with anyone, especially if I'm feeling worried, frustrated, or uncertain. I mind my own business and try not to create additional burdens for other people who already have enough stress in their lives anyway. Plus, if I'm being completely honest, I doubt sometimes whether another person's perspective will really help.

Gradually, however, I've learned that's not necessarily how things look from the perspective of my friends and family. I see myself as independent. They sometimes see me as uncommunicative, hard to read, aloof, and even arrogant. It bothers them that I oftentimes don't want to ask for their help—so gradually, I've learned to ask for it.

Not long ago, I was having trouble writing a newspaper column, and the deadline was rapidly approaching. Over dinner, with these worries very fresh on my mind, I shared my frustrations with my wife and brother. I thought I'd taken the right approach, I told them, but now it was obvious I hadn't. It looked like the column needed a major rewrite, but I had less than two days to do it. There didn't seem to be any way I could go back and get all the new information needed to rework it, and it was too late to start from scratch on a different column.

"Well," my brother said, after my initial burst of complaining had subsided. "I have to say I'm actually glad to see you like this. I was thinking I was the only around here who couldn't figure out his own problems." It felt good to talk about what was on my mind at the moment I was thinking it, instead of after the usual moratorium required for scrubbing and sharpening every word that leaves my mouth. And guess what? Dawn and my brother Jeff listened sympathetically, sorted through potential options, and helped guide me toward a good solution. I headed back to the computer after dinner, and a challenge that had seemed intractable a couple hours before yielded quite easily.

Second, as we open ourselves up to deeper connections with those already closest to us, it's also a good idea to build new friendships with people who are following their callings doggedly. They can inspire and direct us with knowledge gained from the front lines. When I first got to know my neighbor Robin, he was a promising attorney from a high-achieving family of politicians, lawyers, and educators. I envied his pedigree and career prospects, which appeared pretty lucrative. It became evident over time, though, that money, prestige, and conventional career tracks meant little to him. He was far more concerned with making a real difference, especially in the lives of kids. Exactly how he would do that remained murky, however. Early one morning, driving me to the airport for a business trip, he said he'd finally hit on the right idea. Having followed his quest for several years at this point, I could hardly wait to hear it. "My parents might think I'm crazy and my wife will want to strangle me," he said, "but what I really want to be is a public school teacher."

It was not the obvious choice—and certainly not the easy one—for a guy in his mid-thirties with an MBA, law degree, and young family to help support. And yet within a couple months of that conversation, he was teaching social studies at a middle school. He's emerged since then as an outstanding teacher and also a savvy businessman who runs a consulting business on the side to help make ends meet. Most importantly, he feels steeped in a call that makes the constant demands on his time and energy worth it. Sometimes when I find myself wishing for a simpler, clearer-cut role in the world or looking at the stellar résumé of a college classmate who has already left me in the dust professionally (read: financially), I find renewed hope in Robin's example. We all need people like him in our lives to remind us to get on with the business of doing what we feel called to do, regardless of whether it makes sense to anyone else. Hard, inner work is essential for finding and fulfilling a call. We need to zero in on our desires, sharpen our focus, and learn humility. It's work that we ultimately have to do on our own, but we need to get outside of ourselves to do it. Whether we're regularly followed by sportswriters and camera crews like Bob Hurley Sr. or live in complete obscurity like a Trappist monk, the progress we make toward purpose is less about our individual achievements than the challenges we accept and the inspiration and wisdom we gain from our extended community—and what we contribute back to it.

CHAPTER SEVEN

The Margins: Probing Your Potential

BACK IN THE FALL OF 2005, I MADE PLANS FOR A short trip to Jersey City, where my employer was holding a leadership conference. I didn't want to go. My wife had severely sprained her ankle a month before and had just gotten clearance from her doctor to drive. My absence meant she'd have to deal with her job and our whirling dervish of a one-year-old son on just one good leg. In another month, I would be taking an eighteen-hour nonstop flight to Singapore on a business trip. Not being a big fan of heights or planes, I wasn't excited about spending a few additional sweaty-palmed hours in the air. The night before departure, a scratching in my throat announcing the imminent arrival of a head cold, added to my good cheer. All in all, it had been awhile since I'd wanted to do something less than make this trip. And, having become acquainted in the previous year with gag-inducing diaper changes and 3:00 a.m. feedings, that was saying something.

Arriving at the hotel the next day, however, I was quite unprepared for the view from my room. Pulling back the curtains, anticipating a standard, dreary urban landscape, I instead found myself looking straight over the river at the skyscrapers of Manhattan. I was thirty-two and hadn't been to New York City since my freshman year of high school. In the years since, I'd read *Bright Lights, Big City*, subscribed to *The New Yorker* and even married a Jersey girl, but I'd never understood what all the fuss was about. I actually took pride, at a time when many of my friends were flocking there, in having made it through my entire twenties without ever setting foot in New York. I was a much better fit, I believed, in a soundless monastery, which seemed a far more virtuous and instructive place, free of vanity, pollution and over-priced pizza. Right at that moment, though, it was hard not to be impressed by New York's muscular skyline. I went out of the hotel, bought a hot dog from a street vendor, and ate it on a bench with a clear view of the Statue of Liberty. Across the river, cars hurtled past, the sun glinted on the office towers, and ferries chugged to and from the Jersey side. I had to admit, rather grudgingly and with the skepticism of a guy who grew up a block from a farm, that there was a raw energy and ambition to this place that I'd underestimated.

By nightfall, I was completely transfixed, gazing out the window at the twinkling lights of the behemoths across the water like a kid lingering outside a toy store. I reworked plans to meet my college buddy Marc in the hotel restaurant for dinner and instead caught a train into the city to see him there. The abbreviated tour he offered stoked my enthusiasm even more. A couple months earlier I'd started a long-delayed essay on my old college mentor, Wallace

Fowlie, only to see my progress stall. Looking out the hotel window, I recalled Fowlie's love of New York, where in younger days he'd regularly taught literature classes, and suddenly understood that attraction far more clearly. It was easy to picture him, briefcase in hand, Rimbaud verses in his head, strolling through Central Park envisioning his next book, powered by the energy all around him.

There, in the present moment, I needed some way to funnel the surge of ambition I was feeling, too. So I opened my laptop and sprung headlong into the essay about Fowlie, staying up late, squeezing in short bursts of writing between conference sessions, and waking early to keep going. By the time I got off the plane back in North Carolina, an essay that had taken ten years to start was now halfway done. Within six months it would be published—and a lasting connection with New York that has since become central to my writing pursuits and professional career was ignited. It all started with a reluctant trip to an unfamiliar place.

In his book *Leaders Make the Future*, Bob Johansen, who specializes in identifying unfolding trends in business and society, remarks that game-changing innovations don't come from the mainstream—they're the result of stretching the margins. He's referring mainly to new ideas and products that drive business growth. But exploring the margins, those unfamiliar places we'd rather not visit because they scare us or might waste our time, is equally crucial for our growth as individuals.

Regardless of age or how far we've advanced in pursuit of a calling, we can never say we've fully realized our vocations. Christians, in fact, can only approach that completeness through death. As long as we're still here, we need to keep demanding more of ourselves. We must push out, or allow ourselves to be pulled, into the white space—the unexplored terrain of our world and our psyches—for reminders that we tend to underestimate our potential. It's an appropriate exercise, too, because Christianity itself emerged entirely from the margins. Starting out as a tiny sect in an obscure corner of the Roman Empire, it grew precisely because it spoke not to the wealthy and well connected but directly to people in the margins—the faceless laborers and outcasts, the poor, and the imprisoned. It's instructive that Jesus did not go looking for disciples in the best schools, temples, and business enterprises of the day. Their inhabitants were too invested in the status quo. Instead, he found the savvy and courage needed to spread the Gospel among disenfranchised women, poor fishermen, and tax collectors.

◦◦◦

Plateaus are an inevitable part of our journey toward calling, and I had hit one around the time of my arrival in Jersey City. Seriously embracing our desires and following through with focus, humility, and community can take us a long way, and I'd been committed to those practices for years. But they can't take us all the way into our callings. Like monks who battle the "noonday demon" of boredom and distraction, our minds will wander from time to time, and our momentum will slow. When it does, we need a jolt of inspiration to get us refocused. That's what margins provide. Mother Teresa, after all, was deeply committed to her calling as a schoolteacher. There would have been no shame in her living out the rest of her life that way.

Mother Teresa was, however, capable of much more than she or anyone else thought. Fulfilling that potential required hearing a call from the margins—in her case, a direct request from Jesus—and then literally moving into the margins, which for her were the gutters of Calcutta. What an inspiration the world would have missed if she had decided, "Well, this personal appeal from Christ sounds a little extreme. It's probably better if I get the next train back to Delhi and forget about it." But how often in our own lives do we hop onto that very same train, speeding back toward a predictable existence, a calling that has become a bit too comfortable?

There are many routes by which we can enter into the margins—both inside ourselves and out in the wider world. There's physical experience—learning from and about communities and ways of life completely foreign to us. This is what St. Francis did when he left the finery of his family home to eke out an existence in a crumbling church and cave outside of Assisi. There are the margins of emotion, in which certain experiences overturn the bedrock of assumptions on which we've based our lives and rattle our identities to the core. That is the territory into which Dorothy Day was led by the birth of her daughter, whose arrival caused her to question much of what she had previously taken for granted about love and religion. Finally, there are spiritual trials through which our faith is put to a strenuous test, challenging us to assess and affirm what it is we really believe. The most classic example of this, of course, is Jesus Christ in Gethsemane, his soul stretched to the absolute limits of its strength, devastated by his impending fate, and wondering till the very end whether he might yet avoid it.

At various times in our lives, we can encounter the three types of margins simultaneously, and we benefit from exposure to all of them. Indeed, monks live in the margins at several levels. In physical terms, there's the monastery itself, often tucked away on a quiet piece of land, cut off from society, and with little access to family, friends, or the news of the outside world. There are the modest meals, early rising, and profound silence, all creating an environment that can be unnerving in its otherness to even casual visitors. At an emotional level, monks must contend with all they are giving up—love, sex, careers, travel—to follow a path that does not make a lot of sense to most people and where progress can be especially tricky to judge.

Spiritually, monks are tested constantly by the boredom, doubt, and all the petty jealousies, disagreements, and rivalries that inevitably spring up in any community and especially those in which you are bound to the same people for decades. Life in these margins, harrowing though it can be, molds monks into better versions of themselves, shaking up their assumptions, challenging them to know themselves and God more deeply, and endowing them with wisdom they would not have earned otherwise.

Those of us out in the workaday world can also be transformed by our encounters in the margins. And when it comes to the physical ones, there's no better exemplar of their power than Cory Booker. Widely known as the mayor who has led an astonishing revitalization of Newark, New Jersey, Booker seems like the kind of guy whose calling was preordained. He has drawn attention to his city's turnaround through a friendly, well-publicized feud with late-show host Conan O'Brien. Working in tandem with Oprah Winfrey, he persuaded Facebook founder Mark Zuckerberg to contribute $100 million of his personal fortune to Newark's public schools.

Following President Obama's election, Booker was offered the chance to run the White House Office of Urban Affairs Policy—but turned it down to stay focused on Newark. Under Booker's leadership, Newark's crime rate has dropped substantially, the city's leaders have lured hundreds of millions of dollars in private philanthropy and commercial investments, increased safe, affordable housing, and strengthened the city's long-beleaguered finances. All of the credit, of course, does not go to Booker, but he has been a primary catalyst for these achievements—and his successes started squarely in the margins.

Booker had the kind of résumé that made it possible to do anything he wanted. A standout football player at Stanford, where he also excelled in the classroom, he volunteered for a suicide hotline and worked regularly with youth. Booker won a prestigious Rhodes scholarship to Oxford University and later attended Yale Law School. His parents had been executives at IBM, and he easily could have pursued a lucrative corporate career of his own. Booker wanted something different, though, feeling drawn toward a life of service but still unsure of how to apply his talents.

"I was pretty firm on what I didn't want do, but I still didn't know how to manifest the desires I had," he said. "I had a choice of going down a more traditional route or going my own way. I decided to invent myself." He started with a single audacious question: "What would be the wildest dream for myself—the largest thing that I could do that would make me feel that sense of fulfillment and contribution?"[1] His ultimate answer—help an entire community remake itself. Forsaking a high-flying legal career, he instead moved into one of the worst public-housing projects in Newark with the goal of helping turn it around. It was an experiment that started humbly.

Residents, who had seen well-intentioned do-gooders lose faith before, were suspicious of his commitment. Worse, a drug dealer personally threatened to kill him. Partnering with a tenant president, who educated him on what it really took to succeed in this fight, he began the slow work of meeting his neighbors and building a coalition for change. Gradually, good things happened, including the removal of a nearby crack house and the conviction of a slum lord who dominated the neighborhood. Making further progress meant getting support from the city government. When that help wasn't forthcoming, Booker's friends urged him to run for city council—launching his sensational political career.

Booker's example underscores an important truth about living in the margins: they are best navigated incrementally. Booker had big dreams when he moved into the Brick Towers project, but he also understood that fulfilling them meant taking baby steps. So he edged forward one conversation at a time. Certainly, he didn't start out with ambitions of becoming Newark's mayor. In fact, he was very reluctant to run even for a seat on the city council. A campaign would distract him from the deeply meaningful and increasingly successful work he was doing in the housing complex, not to mention it would force him to give up the fellowship that had provided his income. He agonized over what to do. Finally, friends convinced him it was the logical and necessary next step on the journey he had undertaken with them. "Are you here to do what you want to do or to meet the needs of the community?" one person asked him at a decisive moment.[2]

Booker ran for office and wound up unseating a long-time incumbent. Once on the council, he quickly discovered the city's corrupt political machine would prevent real change—so he ran for mayor. He lost a brutal campaign in 2002, founded a grassroots civic program in the city to continue lobbying for reforms, and then made a successful bid for mayor in 2006. "My life has been one long path," he said. "There are days when I get punched and knocked down, but I get up again and keep walking. The path has led in directions that I could never have anticipated."[3] It did not matter, in other words, that Booker was never sure exactly where the margins would lead. It was more important that he was willing to iterate, to stay flexible with his plans and adapt to the opportunities that arose.

Most of us are neither inclined nor particularly well positioned, if we have families and other responsibilities, to explore the physical margins as intensely as Booker. Still, we benefit greatly from venturing into them in some manner, into places that unsettle, challenge, and surprise us. At the outset, it's helpful to remember this: the types of settings that constitute the margins will vary greatly for each one of us. New York, though about as mainstream as a place can get, represented the margins to me. Setting foot there, against my wishes, unlocked a sense of real ambition that had lain dormant since high school.

A decade before the New York trip, my first retreat to a Trappist monastery exercised a similar effect, introducing the startling notion that prayer is a vocation in itself. What can embracing the physical margins look like in your life? It might not require going very far at all, perhaps across town to a food pantry or into a college classroom or to the house of a neighbor you've never gotten to know. The key thing is that you feel a little unsure of yourself, a little uncertain of what will happen next, and that, whatever it turns out to be, you are at least open to learning from it.

Openness, in fact, is central to embracing the emotional margins, where the very core of our identities can be thrown into disarray, challenging us to see ourselves and the very meaning of life in entirely new ways. During a Catholicism course I took in my final semester at Duke, a guest speaker was announced one afternoon. Into the room bounded a boyish-faced Jesuit priest with a big mop of hair and even greater enthusiasm. He'd been, by his own admission, the life of the party during his wild undergraduate days at Duke. Then he underwent a swift, stunning conversion. When he showed up in our classroom, he'd been out of prison for less than a year for his role in a peace protest at a US Air Force base. His name was John Dear, and he was one of the most controversial people I'd ever met.

Since graduating from Duke fourteen years earlier, Dear had become a prolific writer and global advocate for peace and nonviolence, racking up one arrest after another as he protested nuclear weapons and lobbied for social justice. Once nearly kicked out of the Jesuit order for his activism, he infuriated bureaucrats, military brass, and rank-and-file Church members alike with his relentless questioning of the United States military.

Dear spoke a bit of his unlikely evolution from party boy to priest, but it was only years later when I read Dear's autobiography, *A Persistent Peace*, that it became clear what a powerful role the margins played in his conversion. At the start of his junior year at Duke, Dear, looking for an easy class to offset the more rigorous ones on his schedule, signed up for a course on abnormal psychology, then regarded as one of the easiest at the university. The professor offered extra credit to students who agreed to do some volunteer work at local psychiatric clinics and homeless shelters. Dear signed up immediately and soon found himself thrust into the physical margins—in the form of a forbidding state mental hospital.

On his first visit to the hospital, Dear spent a six-hour shift in a room with fifty men, all of them drugged, nearly catatonic, and declared insane after being found guilty of various crimes. Initially terrified for his own safety, Dear struck up conversations with several of the men and spent the day listening to their stories. He writes that by the time he left, "My complacency had been shattered. How could these people be left to rot? . . . When I arrived back at the fraternity house, the party was well under way. I stood among the country's first and best, having just left the least and worst, and the contrast hit me hard: how could humanity be so divided?"[4] Just this brief introduction to the physical margins had catapulted Dear into the emotional ones.

Making weekly visits for the rest of the semester, Dear befriended a psychiatric patient named Diana. Friendly and cheerful, "she seemed to be the only sane person in the institution," Dear writes. "She welcomed me, toured me around, and facilitated my interactions with others." The day after Thanksgiving in 1979, Dear went out to the hospital for his regular visit. But he couldn't find Diana. Asking around, he was led to a suicide-watch room where Diana had been placed after a breakdown. "There she was, lying on the floor, drugged, naked, and crying. She didn't recognize me," he recalls. "I walked through the fraternity door that night, the party in full swing: kegs full of beer, stereo blasting, couples necking on the benches outside. Suddenly all of it—the way we lived as if nothing mattered—revolted and grieved me."[5]

It was a crucial turning point for Dear, whose entire world was rocked by the experience. He'd been satisfied before to be a frat guy and talented musician who dreamed of a career in music. All of a sudden he didn't know who he was or what he wanted. His search for answers first led him into nihilistic despair before slowly returning him to the Catholic faith of his youth, which he embraced this time with a totally new sense of seriousness, curiosity, and urgency. By the end of his junior year, exploring the margins had led Dear directly to his calling: he wanted to become a Jesuit priest.

Just as Booker's example reminds us that thriving in the margins often means proceeding incrementally, Dear shows us that making room in our lives for reflection is equally important. The radically new experiences we often encounter in the margins can greatly accelerate our journey toward calling—but only if we pause long enough to make sense of them. It's very regrettable, in the words of poet T. S. Eliot, to have the experience but miss the meaning, and yet this happens all the time in our lives. It would have been easy enough for Dear, once the semester and his trips to the mental hospital ended, to forget about the whole thing. Instead, he devoted time right away, on the rides back to campus from the hospital and alone in his dorm room, to thinking about what he'd seen. His intense introspection first led Dear to reject God, as he pondered the suffering and injustices around him and wondered how an almighty creator could allow them. Ultimately unable to stomach his own depressing conclusion that life was meaningless, he gave faith one more try. He enrolled in a couple courses that fortuitously connected him with Duke's Catholic student community and also introduced him to the struggles and achievements of the great American educator and contemplative St. Elizabeth Ann Seton. Without doing the hard work of sorting through his painful, inner conflicts, feeling them deeply and then acting on what he learned, Dear might have missed his calling entirely.

The task of finding time to think, even briefly, about our own experiences in the margins has not gotten any easier in the three decades since Dear's conversion. Bombarded by text messages, e-mails, and phone calls at all hours of the day, not to mention the lure of the Internet and cable television, it's quite common these days to exist in a state of permanent distraction. When we have a notable experience out in the margins, we need to be very deliberate about carving out time to reflect on it right away, or we risk losing its meaning altogether. I knew, for example, that my trip to Jersey City needed to be examined swiftly, before I got swept up in the routines of the office and family life. My preferred method of reflection involves journal writing and note taking, so I quickly made time for that—and confirmed that the swell of ambition I'd felt there was a strong hint that I wasn't challenging myself enough. Soon after, I enrolled in graduate school and also started writing more demanding essays. At other times, though, when I've attended conferences or met someone intriguing or completed an interesting project at work, I haven't set aside time for reflection—and essentially nothing has come of it. For people who are less inclined to write, reflection might involve chatting with a trusted friend over lunch, praying, or simply going for a quiet run. The method doesn't matter. Making the effort does.

Beyond the physical margins and the emotional ones lies a frontier even more daunting and potentially trans-formative—the spiritual margins. This is the place where our faith is challenged and stretched and forged like never before. It can be terrifying—like the lost connection with God was for Mother Teresa. It can be exhilarating, as was John Dear's sudden conversion. It can leave us baffled, as Dorothy Day discovered during her long, frustrating jour-ney from joining the Church to finding her niche in it with the Catholic Worker movement. Or, it can be all three of those things at once. No one knew that better than Mary. Most of what little we know of her comes from the Gos-pel of Luke. Mary is betrothed to Joseph when the angel Gabriel arrives in Nazareth and tells her she will bear a son named Jesus. Mary is startled by the news but accepts. Not long after, she heads to Judah to visit her kinswoman Elizabeth, who is pregnant with John the Baptist. Elizabeth is overjoyed to see Mary, proclaiming her "the mother of my Lord. " Mary responds with a litany of praise for God. They spend about three months together before Mary heads back to her home.

With a little imagination, we can explore just how far out into the spiritual margins this sequence takes Mary. Luke tells us that Mary "was greatly troubled" upon being greeted by Gabriel, but probably not as troubled as she felt a few moments later when she learned she would bear a child not fathered by Joseph. She must have instantly feared the condemnation that would follow this highly unorthodox pregnancy, partly from her community but even more so from Joseph, who would look to everyone else like a fool who had chosen an unfaithful woman. What would become of her? Beyond that, the fact that she has just spoken with an angel and been selected among all the women who ever lived to be the mother of God's son must have been virtually impossible to comprehend. This is a severe test of faith, and, because Mary was initially frightened by Gabriel's appearance, as any of us would be, it appears she has not been granted super-human capacities for dealing with it. She is, in the end, a young girl in an out-of-the-way place who has just been asked to accept on faith something totally unprecedented, something that will complicate her life in ways too numerous to count. These are spiritual margins of the farthest extreme, unknown, really, to anyone else in history. Still, rather than asking questions or hesitating, she tells Gabriel, "Behold, I am the handmaid of the Lord; let it be to me according to your word." It's an extraordinary statement—one difficult to utter at even the most mundane moments of our lives.

Cory Booker demonstrates the importance of working our way through the margins patiently and flexibly. John Dear reminds us that reflection plays a crucial role as we go along. These are both approaches that we can, to a great extent, initiate and control ourselves. We are in the driver's seat. However, in affirming to Gabriel that she welcomes his news, Mary models another trait that is essential for navigating the margins: a willingness to let ourselves be led by circumstance, to see the very place in which we are now as precisely where God wants us to be and to show our faith by embracing it. Certainly, it's not easy. Initially, Mary accepts what is asked of her matter-of-factly. It's hard to imagine her doing anything else, stunned as she must have been. She needs time to absorb what has just happened before she can enter into it fully. I like to envision her trekking in silence up into the dusty hills to visit Elizabeth, a journey that would have taken several days and given her plenty of time to think and pray. By the time she arrives at Elizabeth's house, she has moved from fear and bafflement to exhilaration. "My soul magnifies the Lord, and my spirit rejoices in God my Savior," Mary tells Elizabeth, beginning her Magnificat that joyfully exalts God's power and mercy. Rather than resisting a situation that caught her completely off guard, which would have been totally understandable, Mary finds a way to align herself with it. It doesn't happen right away. She needs time and presumably lots of prayer. But she gets out of her own way and finds her soul elevated as never before.

A streak of independence and willfulness can serve us well in the margins, fueling us with initiative and persistence. Certainly neither Booker nor Dear, nor Mary for that matter, would have made it very far without those qualities. But how do we then dial back our self-sufficiency at the appropriate times and let ourselves be led instead? How can we, in small ways at least, honor the example of Mary? For one thing, we can make it a habit to look for God and holiness in all circumstances, especially the ordinary ones. Br. Lawrence spent most of his life as a lowly cook in a seventeenth-century French monastery. He didn't have much education or great connections or a dazzling mind— and yet he is remembered as one of Christianity's great spiritual masters. His central insight is the importance of shaping every single thing we do into an act of praise, whether it is cooking meals, talking with friends, or, to paraphrase him, picking a piece of straw off the ground.

How we handle the unceasing flow of little moments in our lives prepares us for success with the big ones, like surprise visits from angels. It's highly unlikely Mary would have responded as gracefully had she not already weaved a constant attitude of worship deep into the fabric of her being. We can begin to train ourselves in the same way by approaching chores, for example, not merely as drudgery but as something to be done with mindfulness and gratitude for the breath we have been given to do them. If our first duty is to pray, as St. Paul reminds us, we need to start right where we are and not wait for those rare moments of reverence to come over us. As we embrace moments we would rather race through to get to something better, we gradually teach ourselves how to live in the moment. We learn how to be led. We can join with Br. Lawrence in saying, "Lord of all pots and pans and things, make me a saint by getting meals and washing up the plates!"

Ultimately, living in the margins, if handled effectively, should bring us back to ourselves—centering us far more firmly in our own skin and in our quest to find and fulfill a call. We are in pursuit of bigger hearts in which vocation can take root and thrive, and in this way our goals are the very same as those of monks. "The heart is the monk's turf. His permanent place is between the darkness and the light of the human heart, this region of wound and wisdom, this land called desire . . ." writes Michael Downey. "For there is nothing more central to the task of being and becoming human than the full flourishing of the heart's yearning."[6] It is precisely that yearning that stirs us out of complacency, that gives us glimpses of the margins we might yet occupy in our worlds and our souls. Going out to explore them is alternately disorienting and thrilling—and a natural, necessary next step in the vocational journey. We won't venture into these fringes alone, after all. If we have prepared properly, we go with a stronger sense of our desires, greater focus, enough humility to know what we don't know, and a community of friends and family who are rooting for and ready to support us. We go as monks go, with hearts full of expectation.

Holy Ambition: Sustaining What You Start

DEEP INTO *THE SUN ALSO RISES*, ERNEST HEMING-way's classic novel about hapless expatriates drinking their way through 1920s Europe, narrator Jake Barnes, intoxicated, sleepless, and lovesick in a Pamplona hotel room, takes stock of his exceedingly messy—and increasingly meaningless—life. "I did not care what it was all about. All I wanted to know was how to live in it," Barnes muses. "Maybe if you found out how to live in it you learned from that what it was all about."[1] In that moment, despite his disarray, Barnes hits on an essential truth about vocation: it's more important to get on to the field in pursuit of a call than to try grasping it solely in our heads from the sidelines. Of course, I had read this novel and Barnes's advice when I was eighteen and again when I was twenty-one. It never stuck. At those ages and well beyond them, I believed that I couldn't possibly live life fully without knowing first what the whole point of it was. And so I endlessly asked myself and some unfortunate souls who happened to be nearby, "What is it exactly that I'm supposed to do?"—convinced that my life would not really start until that answer somehow arrived.

The practical implications of that mindset were poisonous. I grew paralyzed, unwilling to commit to romantic relationships unless every element looked perfect, rejecting a series of potential careers without actually testing any of them, delaying even modest efforts to exercise and improve my diet until I had a comprehensive fitness plan worked out. It was only when I settled rather chaotically into a career in writing, married Dawn, and started taking care of myself physically that a sense of vocation gradually began to reveal itself. Barnes was right—by living in it, we really do give ourselves a chance to learn what it's all about.

In searching for a vocation, we won't start out with many answers. There is something more important, however, that we do need in order to thrive in this pursuit—ambition. It's a dirty word in some ways, one that calls to mind selfishness and unethical single-mindedness, the no-holds-barred pursuit of money and possessions, an excuse for trampling over everything that gets in the way of our goals. Gordon Gekko, the anti-hero stockbroker of Oliver Stone's *Wall Street* movies, is ambitious. Politicians who will say and do whatever it takes to win an election are ambitious. Some of the most ruthless leaders throughout history, from Genghis Khan to Pol Pot, were exceedingly so as well. But St. Francis of Assisi was ambitious, too, as were Ignatius of Loyola, Mother Teresa, Dorothy Day, and, in fact, just about every individual profiled in this book. They remind us that there is a counterpoint to worldly ambition—holy ambition, a powerful and positive drive to transform ourselves and the world around us.

Msgr. Anthony Marcaccio, the pastor of my parish church in North Carolina, likes to talk about the dangers of complacency in the spiritual life. When it comes to prayer and service, he says, it's alarmingly easy to fall into a routine with which we're comfortable—and then, gradually, far too much at ease. We need to demand more of ourselves. "Jesus doesn't say, 'Could you please, please become mediocre,'" Marcaccio told me. "Everyone has the potential to be a saint, and I have met many of them in my life as a priest."

We won't get there, of course, without taking regular stock of what we're doing to nurture a relationship with God and to live it out in concrete ways. We constantly need to challenge ourselves, to zero in on the next steps we can take in service of faith, regardless of our age, station in life, or previous accomplishments.

The same goes for uncovering our vocations. Probing our desires, sharpening our focus, developing humility, embracing community, and exploring the margins are crucial practices. But all of that work, in each of its stages, is more of a journey than an event. Our efforts with the five practices are never entirely complete, because the circumstances within which we exercise them keep changing. We start a career. We get married. We have children. We change jobs, perhaps many times. We grow older and lose family members and friends. We find new passions. We need to revisit those practices again and again, building on everything we have learned along the way. Staying alive to our opportunities and challenges calls for a healthy sense of ambition, a belief that we can keep changing for the better.

The examples of the seekers in these pages offer a couple key truths about vocation that are worth reminding ourselves of frequently. First—and this one eluded me for a long time—we can and absolutely should cultivate more than one vocation at a time. In all likelihood, there isn't one single thing we are intended to do with our lives, and we can save ourselves a lot of time and distress by simply accepting that reality. It's liberating, frankly, to discover our callings can be multifaceted; we're freed from obsessing over that one needle in the haystack and just might begin to discover several more valuable ones as we dig through the straw. Dorothy Day searched relentlessly through her twenties and into her thirties for the work that would fill her tremendous appetite for meaning. In the end, it turned out fulfillment for her depended on simultaneously cultivating several callings as a Catholic, mother, journalist, and groundbreaking promoter of social justice—all of them working together to form one massive canvas of significance.

Second, our vocations will probably not remain static; they are very likely to shift over time. Some core elements of a calling might stay the same. Mother Teresa, for example, always felt called to serve the Church. Exactly how she did that, however, changed dramatically as she evolved from an obscure school teacher to a fearless advocate for Calcutta's poor, to a revered international symbol of charity and selfless service. Her prayer life itself changed, too, from rather conventional worship to an intense, complex, and very intimate relationship with Jesus that plummeted from brief rapture to extended, aching darkness before leveling into an uneasy peace. We, too, are likely to experience changes in how we define our calls as we experiment with different careers, raise families, endure hardships and disappointments, and unearth unexpected talents and interests.

In sustaining what we start on the journey of vocation, monastic wisdom comes once again to our aid. Monks are elite athletes of vocation, and their approach to fulfilling the calls they identify bears study and repeating. Perhaps most importantly, the Trappists I've observed embrace their mission with an inspiring wholeheartedness that is refreshingly free of hedging and emergency-escape hatches. Of course they experience doubts and question their trajectory at times, as the journals of Thomas Merton, the most famous American Trappist of all, reveal quite plainly. Still, they take care to root themselves deeply in their callings—at the spiritual level through a series of vows, and at the physical level by agreeing to spend their entire lives at one monastery. For them, monasticism is a lifelong project, and we do well to regard vocation with the same extended perspective. One monk in particular reminded me why.

The gift shop at Mepkin Abbey had bustled all morning with tourists and weekend retreatants like myself. By the time I made it to the checkout line, though, the place was almost empty. There was just me and the man behind the cash register: Br. Stephen, an eighty-ish, bald, wiry guy with a narrow face and a pleasant grin. He rang up my purchases—a few books, some jam, and a box of chocolates from a convent in Mississippi. He asked how I was doing. I told him I hadn't been to Mepkin for a number of years. With a job and a young family, I explained, it wasn't easy to get away. "Work *is* prayer," he told me. And so, he added, is raising small children. Images of home—floors strewn with an ankle-turning array of toys, Cheerios cemented to the wall—flashed before me. Cleaning that up counted as prayer? It doesn't matter what you're doing, Br. Stephen said, as long as you're trying to think of God while you do it. That's what the monks at Mepkin did whether they were singing in the choir, cooking breakfast, or slipping boxes of chocolates into paper bags. Our relationship with God is the only reality that counts. "That's all there is," Br. Stephen said with a strength of conviction that I've rarely heard in anyone's voice. "There's nothing else."

I instantly admired and envied Br. Stephen's wisdom and remarkable comfort in his own skin. In the monastic pecking order, he wasn't anything special. He hadn't been ordained as a priest or served the monastery in senior leadership roles. But he was clearly a sage, and his knowledge had accrued over decades. If we'd had the chance to talk more, I'm sure he would have described struggles he endured over the years. I'm sure, too, he would have explained that simply believing in the purpose he had found and sticking with it, especially during the times he felt least like hanging in there, had made all the difference. That brings us to another truth about living out our vocations: we need to prepare for the mundane, uninspiring stretches on our journey—because there will be many of them. Finding and fulfilling a vocation, as our guides throughout history have shown us, is a marvelous adventure. There's the thrill of latching onto something that matters deeply to us. There's the delight of finding we are capable of more than we thought. We might even experience extraordinary breakthroughs akin to St. Francis kissing the leper. Most of our lives, though, will be the opposite, consumed with routine activities that will at least occasionally grate on our nerves. That dynamic, which becomes apparent pretty early in our lives, doesn't change just because we have discovered a deeper purpose. Monks know this well. As Mepkin Abbey's Fr. Aelred Hagan has noted about monastic life, "Everything you will ever do here, you will have done in your first six months in the monastery."[2]

Monks do not seek out listlessness and boredom, but they don't flee from them either. Indeed, learning how to work through ordinary moments prayerfully and mindfully is one of the keys to realizing their vocation. Michael Downey writes that "staying alive to the monastic life entails finding the sacred not only in choir while chanting the psalms and in the celebration of the Eucharist and in the shared life of the brothers and in lectio divina, but even and especially when not much seems to be happening. In the doldrums. On Wednesday afternoon."[3] This is precisely where the monastic vows of stability pay dividends. By putting down roots in one place, monks stand still long enough to spot patterns and measure progress beneath a daily grind that might otherwise seem devoid of meaning.

Were monks to bounce from one monastery to the next in search of something new and exciting, they would never scratch beyond the surface of any of them. In the same way, if we have dedicated ourselves to the practices in this book and arrived at an authentic calling, we need to remain committed to it. Cory Booker had many occasions, whether it was slogging through long, tedious neighborhood meetings, sleeping in a dreary apartment, or shaking the hand of yet another skeptical voter, when he might have walked away from the housing project into which he voluntarily moved in Newark. He could have taken his Yale law degree and Rhodes scholarship and claimed a high-end lifestyle in an instant.

Like a good monk, however, Booker held his ground, began to see beneath the surface to what made his community tick, and figured out ways to change it. His is a glorious vocation, but it's built of everyday nuts and bolts. "So many of us are inclined to imagine that we are destined for big things, and so our lives seem to us one big disappointment," Downey writes. "We live in a prolonged state of disillusionment. We might even get lost in fantasy: Perhaps I'll join a monastery! A great life indeed. Heroic. But it is a life never greater or more adventuresome or self-sacrificing than on Wednesday afternoon."[4]

We must balance holy ambition, in other words, with modesty. Vocation is a lifelong process, and we should pace ourselves accordingly, accepting that this journey will be characterized by a great deal of drudgery that is lightened at unpredictable moments by penetrating insights and a powerful sense of rightness. Ambition compels us to steep ourselves in the five vocational practices, but modesty reminds us the practices themselves cannot be attained by working through a checklist—and that developing facility in them is not an end in itself. Just as we can become consumed with raising our children or advancing our career to the point we lose all perspective, we can also become too wrapped up in the mechanics of vocation, regarding it is as the mother of all projects and one that will end happily only if we work at it feverishly and without rest. Thomas Merton watched many people cripple their spiritual lives by misperceiving what God required of them: "Blinded by their desire for ceaseless motion, for a constant sense of achievement, famished with a crude hunger for results, for visible and tangible success, they work themselves into a state in which they cannot believe that they are pleasing

God unless they are busy with a dozen jobs at the same time."[5] The same can happen in our pursuit of calling.

Emerging from the throes of my anxiety disorder and eager to find a driving purpose, I succumbed in similar fashion. Aiming for structure after years without much of it, I made a list of the top priorities on which I would ideally spend my time. It looked something like this—faith, family, fitness, career, friends, reading, writing, and volunteer service. Ever earnest and more than a bit naive, I made a chart to measure my progress, which also seemed logical. Then came the big error: deciding that a day would not count as a success unless I'd done something in nearly all of those areas. You can imagine what happened. It was impossible to do justice to more than a few of these catego ries in a single day, much less all of them. By evening, I'd be frustrated and would try to cram in everything at once, glancing at a book as I talked to a friend on the phone while, in another corner of my mind, plotting out my next work day. A recipe for mindfulness this was not. Gradually, realizing the scales had tipped almost exclusively toward ambition at modesty's expense, I shifted from a manic-checklist mentality to a more balanced, reflective approach. My priorities stayed the same and, in fact, are basically the same today. The difference is progress is not measured on a daily basis. Every quarter or so, instead, I'll take a little time and assess what I've been up to in each of these areas, recognizing they all play key roles in my evolving vocation and need nurturing over time, if not exactly the same time. Modest, incremental efforts can add up significantly over the long haul.

Indeed, an ability to maintain the long view counts among the greatest strengths of monks. In seeking God, they undertake a mission without a clear end point and few conventional markers of success. It's a journey in which success is hard to gauge on any kind of near-term basis and wisdom accrues very slowly, over decades—a path entirely like the ones the rest of us walk, or crawl, every day. Perhaps the vagaries of the experience do not bother monks too much because they draw on and judge their work against a tradition that stretches back nearly two thousand years to the early desert fathers. We, by contrast, live in an age that pummels us relentlessly with torrents of information, demanding short-term responses and favoring instant gratification. E-mails pile up, Facebook updates flow in constantly, the cable company adds another ten channels to the two thousand we had already.

It's increasingly possible—in some ways, nearly unavoidable—to move through life without much mindfulness or reflection, without the spadework that prepares the way for lasting vocations. Monasticism reminds us to pay attention to the larger arc of our own stories, to embrace our lives as a narrative still in progress, a tale that will by turns grow frustrating, jubilant, frightening, energizing, and, ultimately, redemptive. The point is not to write perfect chapters from the very start or to become obsessed with starting over. We are called to proceed from where we are right now, in all of our messiness, relying on grace and our own patient, steady efforts to guide us along.

Acknowledgments

THE MESSY PROCESS OF WRITING THIS BOOK MADE one thing quite clear: the finished product belongs as much to others as it does to me. Its contents are a reflection of what I've been privileged to learn over thirty-nine years from a wonderfully wise and giving community of family, friends, teachers, coworkers and fellow writers.

Two individuals, without whom this project would never have gotten off the ground, deserve special recognition—Tim Reidy and Patrick McGowan. Tim, an editor at *America* magazine, has been a treasured advocate and sounding board for the past seven years. He skillfully nurtured in me an interest in writing personal essays that ultimately found fuller expression in this book. I'm grateful for his talent and generosity and, most of all, his friendship. I'm equally indebted to Patrick, my editor at Ave Maria Press, who approached me nearly two years ago about doing a book on calling. Patrick has continually demonstrated an impressive knack for making much more sense out of my thoughts than I can. He's a savvy editor with great instincts for knowing when to push and when to praise. Even as his tough critiques sometimes compelled me to rewrite entire chapters, I found myself laughing out loud at the deadpan wit with which he slashed my beloved paragraphs.

I've been fortunate, too, to be blessed with several excellent mentors over the years whose guidance, example, and confidence in me as a writer has been priceless. Among them: Judy Eby, my fifth grade teacher; Dick Cleary, my high school philosophy teacher; and Bob Bliwise, the longtime editor of Duke's distinguished alumni magazine, where I learned the fundamentals of journalism.

Not every organization would be excited when an employee with a busy day job announces that he'll also be writing a book on the side. But my bosses at the Center for Creative Leadership, namely John Ryan, Portia Mount, and Jeff Howard, have been enthusiastic about this project from the start, and it's hard to overstate the significance of their support. Once the work began, a talented group of friends, several of whom have written books of their own and all of whom offered valuable advice and encouragement, came to my aid. They include Paul Baerman, Justin Catanoso, Shannon Dahlstedt, Emily Freeman, Christopher Gergen, Kyle Kramer, and Karen Smith.

Then there are those who were not as closely involved in the creation of this book but whose enduring friendships and inspiring examples have become so much a part of my worldview that they rank as implicit coauthors whether they like it or not: Jeff Bischoff, Marc Borkan, Patrick Brennan, Kai Chen, Earle Ellis, Mary Harris, Andrew Kapustin, and Courtney Rubin.

Every year I'm more appreciative of my family, which, courtesy of the sprawling Fugini clan, handed along a vibrant Roman Catholic faith and muscular models for living it out in the real world. My mother, Bernadette Martin, is the font of spirituality among the Martins, and the older I get the more I admire her self-sacrifice, good humor and resilience, not to mention her superb spaghetti and meatballs. My father, David Martin, imbued in me a love of travel and all things Duke and, in a tremendous act of generosity, footed the bill for me to study there. Together, they made a home in which books were plentiful, writing was esteemed and my future was up to me. My younger brother Jeff, who survived much pummeling from me during our childhood and later rode out my grim Albert Camus fixation with remarkable grace, is a gifted writer and teacher and irreplaceable confidante.

Finally, there's the closest group of all—the three people who lived with me as I wrote this book: my wife Dawn and our children Evan and Elly. Dawn and I have been together for fourteen years, and I find her more beguiling every day. She's fun, honest, loving, and smarter than I am—best of all, she still doesn't realize it. She's also been the biggest fan of this book, providing kind words, savvy edits, and time to get it done. My journey toward vocation began in earnest the day that we met. Evan, seven, and Elly, four, also excel at changing my life for the better—and they don't realize it either. Their curiosity, enthusiasm and sweetness exist in such abundance that they might have even rubbed off a bit on their dad. I wish for them the greatest gift of all—a path toward calling richly strewn with messiness and meaning.

Notes

Chapter One

1. Carlo Carretto, *Letters from the Desert* (Maryknoll, NY: Orbis Books, 2002), 60.
2. Fyodor Dostoyevsky, *Crime and Punishment* (New York: Penguin, 1980).
3. Thomas Merton, *New Seeds of Contemplation* (New York: New Directions Books, 1972), 239.

Chapter Two

1. James Martin, S.J., *Becoming Who You Are* (Mahwah, NJ: Hidden Spring, 2006), 17.
2. Michael Downey, *Trappist* (Mahwah, NJ: Paulist Press, 1997), 162.
3. Ibid., 164.

Chapter Three

1. Maureen Parker, "Earth Scholar," *News & Record*, April 22, 2007, news-record/content/2008/06/27/article/why_do_we_suffer_the_answer_is_a_mystery.
2. James Martin, S.J., *The Jesuit Guide to Almost Everything* (New York: HarperCollins, 2010), 61.
3. Francis Kline, O.C.S.O., *Four Ways of Holiness for the Universal Church* (Kalamazoo, MI: Cistercian Publications, 2007), 76.
4. Downey, *Trappist*, 70.
5. Martin Sheen, interview by Garrison Keillor, *A Prairie Home Companion*, September 29, 2007.
6. Peter Drucker, "Managing Oneself," *Harvard Business Review*, January 2005, hbr.org/2005/01/managing-oneself/ar/1.
7. Bob Johansen, *Leaders Make the Future* (San Francisco: Berrett-Koehler 2009), 158–59.
8. Parker Palmer, *Let Your Life Speak* (San Francisco: Jossey-Bass, 1999), 46.
9. Ibid., 60.

10. Dorothy Day, *The Long Loneliness* (San Francisco: HarperCollins, 1952), 139.

11. Ibid., 148.

12. Lenos Trigeorgis, Rainer Brosch, Han Smit, "Stay Loose," *Wall Street Journal*, September 14, 2007.

Chapter Four

1. Tony Schwartz, *The Way We're Working Isn't Working* (New York: Free Press, 2010), 33.

2. Ibid., 36.

3. Ibid., 38.

4. Francis Kline, O.C.S.O., *Lovers of the Place* (Collegeville, MN: The Liturgical Press, 1997), 33.

5. Cardinal Joseph Bernardin, *The Gift of Peace* (New York: Doubleday, 1997), 5.

6. Ibid.

7. Robert Ellsberg, *All Saints* (New York: Crossroad Publishing, 2000), 495.

8. Schwartz, *The Way We're Working Isn't Working*, 39.

9. Van Biema, "Mother Teresa's Crisis of Faith," *TIME*, August 23, 2007, www.time.com/time/magazine/article/0,9171,1655720,00.html.

10. Carol Zaleski, "The Dark Night of Mother Teresa," *First Things*, May 2003, www.firstthings.com/article/2007/08/the_dark_night_of_mother_terersa_42.

11. Van Biema, "Mother Teresa's Crisis of Faith."

12. Ibid.

13. Marshall Goldsmith, *What Got You Here Won't Get You There* (New York: Hyperion, 2007), 195.

Chapter Five

1. Hilary Spurling, *Matisse the Master: The Conquest of Colour, 1909–1954* (London: Alfred A. Knopf, 2005), 449.

2. Ibid., 455.

3. Susan A. Sternau, *Henri Matisse* (Singapore: New Line Books, 2005), 119.

4. Ibid., 119.

5. Walter Ciszek, S.J., *He Leadeth Me* (San Francisco: Ignatius Press, 1973), 21.

6. Markus Hofer, *Francis For Men*, trans. by Sharon Therese Nemeth (Cincinnati: St. Anthony Messenger Press, 2003), 16.

7. Ibid., 21.

8. Ellsberg, *All Saints*, 428.

Chapter Six

1. David Brooks, "The Arduous Community," *New York Times*, December 20, 2010.
2. Erica Brown, "Working Together," leadingwithmeaning.com. (accessed Nov. 26, 2011).
3. Ibid.
4. Bob Hurley, "Bob Hurley, the Sage of St. Anthony," interview by Steve Kroft, *60 Minutes*, March 27, 2011.
5. Downey, *Trappist*, 140.
6. Ibid., 24.

Chapter Seven

1. Christopher Gergen and Gregg Vanourek, *Life Entrepreneurs* (San Francisco: Jossey-Bass, 2008), 26.
2. Ibid., 27.
3. Ibid., 28.
4. John Dear, S.J., *A Persistent Peace* (Chicago: Loyola Press, 2008), 13.
5. Ibid., 15.
6. Downey, *Trappist*, 152–53.

Conclusion

1. Ernest Hemingway, *The Sun Also Rises* (New York: Macmillan Publishing Co., 1986), 148.
2. Downey, *Trappist*, 140.
3. Ibid., 143.
4. Ibid., 147.
5. Merton, *New Seeds of Contemplation*, 206.

STEPHEN MARTIN is a speech writer, journalist, and award-winning essayist. He directs public relations and executive communications for the nonprofit Center for Creative Leadership. Formerly a business and education reporter for several daily newspapers, Martin coauthors a regular column on social innovation and entrepreneurship for the *Raleigh News & Observer*. His essays have appeared in *America, Commonweal, Portland,* and on washingtonpost.com. He holds a bachelor's degree from Duke University and a master's degree from the University of North Carolina-Greensboro. He and his wife Dawn and their two children live in Greensboro, North Carolina, where they are members of St. Pius X Catholic Church.